The Lemon Golf Diary

Based on a true story

by
Christine Foster

Copyright © 2024, Christine Foster

All rights reserved. No part of this text may be reproduced, stored in a retrieval system or shared or transmitted in any form or by any means – electronic, mechanical, photocopying, and recording or otherwise – without the prior written permission of the author. Any use other than the exception is an infringement of copyright.

ISBN: 978-1-7386603-8-4

Buddha Press Publishing

For my daughter

Contents

Chapter One 7

Chapter Two 11

Chapter Three 17

Chapter Four 23

Chapter Five 27

Chapter Six 31

Chapter Seven 33

Chapter Eight 39

Chapter Nine 43

Chapter Ten 49

Chapter Eleven 53

Chapter Twelve 61

Chapter Thirteen 69

Chapter Fourteen 75

Chapter Fifteen 81

Chapter Sixteen 87

Chapter Seventeen 95

Chapter Eighteen 103

Chapter Nineteen	107
Chapter Twenty	115
Chapter Twenty-One	121
Chapter Twenty-Two	127
Chapter Twenty-Three	135
About The Author	140

Neurodivergence

A normal variation in the human genome offering an alternative but equally authentic and valuable form of creative expression and being.

CHAPTER ONE

There was a young girl of Thermopylae
Who never did anything properly...

I used to think my mother could save me. But she's started to look at me like something she didn't mean to order in a restaurant.

Still, I did peek into the laundry room once when she was folding my clothes. She took my blue hooded sweatshirt out of the dryer and brought it up to her face and held it there. I couldn't see her eyes.

About a year ago she cut out sugar and dyes in my food and put a dreamcatcher over my bed. She tells me not to be afraid - but what I'm most afraid of is that she thinks that I'm normal.

She told me, once, that until children are seven years old, they live with the Gods. She said this is a Japanese saying but she was born in Ireland, so I don't know where she heard it.

I guess she believes this is true because she says that until I was seven, I was a 'storm of sunshine' which I think means she thinks I was a lot better then than she thinks I am now.

For my eleventh birthday she gave me a diary (with lines in it) but I never used it. It's hard for me to write very much when my mind is thinking so many things at once and it was even harder last year.

When she saw I hadn't written anything she gave me an audio recorder because she says she is sure I have a lot of thoughts I don't want to lose.

But I lost the recorder. I'm still hoping it will turn up, but I can't find it anywhere.

Then last week Mr. Cullen, who sometimes lives here, wanted me to bring it outside to record some birds singing. I told him that Paige had borrowed it because I'm still hoping I might find it somewhere. But I can't think where.

Sometimes I don't want to think at all. I'd rather just watch something on television because no one on TV ever gets upset with me. But my mother only lets me watch an hour a day and I'm not allowed to have a phone or a computer of my own, although I can use hers when she's around. She says they are like a kind of Electronic Oz that will suck me into even less reality than I'm in now, and that my concentration will be improved much more by reading books. (Only it's hard to improve your concentration when you can't concentrate.)

Mr. Cullen tells her not to expect too much since I couldn't even read Dr. Seuss by myself until I was seven and I "clearly won't be reading Tolkien anytime soon."

I don't mind him saying things like that as much as I mind him smiling when he says it. Anyway, now because I don't have the recorder, I'm trying to write something in the diary every day. Luckily it doesn't matter when you use it because it doesn't have a year written on the front. Or anywhere inside either.

This diary is a fine idea except I can never write things out, not like telling a story. Although I wish I could because I am in bad trouble. Or I will be if people find out. Sometimes they don't.

So, I will try, even if it's only one sentence a day. It's a start. Like it's starting to be spring now.

March 5th: Until children are seven, they live with the Gods

CHAPTER TWO

Paige is skinny as a dandelion and good at all sorts of things, but she has absolutely no imagination. So, there are really only two reasons why she is my best friend:

One: No one else wants to spend time with her because she is very bossy and acts as if she thinks she's superior, which to be honest, she mostly is.

Two: I have played a horrible trick on her which was horribly easy to pull off because she has no imagination.

Which is how I got into all this trouble.

We first met in the woods behind my house during spring vacation when she'd just moved here from somewhere else.

I was out looking for tracks. There was hardly any snow left so it wasn't working out very well.

There is an old tree with a split trunk you can climb up into. And she was sitting in it when I first saw her.

"Hello," she said, calling down to me. "Welcome to the North Pole."

"Why do you call this the North Pole?"

"I don't know," she shrugged. This is just like her. Ideas come all right, but then they go.

"Do you live around here?" I asked.

"Over the other side of the woods."

"So, you'll be going to Franklin Park?"

"Is that where you go?"

I nodded, "I live right up there. Do you want to come and have something to eat?"

"No. I'm going home now," she said, jumping down and checking her phone. (She is allowed to have a phone, but she only uses it to call home. This is her rule, not her mother's. She says that only weak-minded people spend time on Instagram and Tik Tok. This is another example of her superiority.)

But then she switched it off and looked like she wasn't in a hurry after all. "What do you call it then? This tree?"

"I call it the Gods and Goddesses Tree."

"Why?"

"I like myths and things."

She just stared at me and blinked.

So I wasn't sure I should tell her this, but it wasn't boasting since it was true. "And my name's the same as the Goddess of the Dawn. Aurora. Rory for short."

"Sounds like a boy's name." Her lip curled up a bit, then uncurled right away, as she brightened. "Hey, we could make this our meeting place. See you tomorrow?"

And by the time we started back at school we were getting together every Saturday.

We had Ms. Seaton until she left to have her baby. She always used to talk really fast, like she couldn't wait for three o'clock to come. And when I couldn't finish - or sometimes even start - something she wanted me to do, her voice would start squeaking like a rusty seat on an old Ferris wheel and all of my muscles would get so tense that even though I looked and looked at blackboard I couldn't make out a single word. My mother took me to the eye doctor a couple of months ago, but he said there was nothing wrong with my eyes.

One day I put my hand up because I thought maybe the answer was 'dolphins.' She just took a big, slow breath and said no, that wasn't what she was asking at all, and did I know the real answer or not? I could only whisper that I guess I didn't, and she rolled her eyes and muttered, "No, of course you don't."

I thought the other kids would snigger because it wasn't totally under her breath this time, but for some reason they just looked away.

After Easter though we had Ms. Patel, who is a lot better.

Anyway, as soon as Paige was introduced around, she just stood off to one side at breaks and watched everyone. Some of the boys played dodgeball but since most of the kids had phones they just stood around in small groups. Jasmine and Mikayla weren't allowed to bring theirs to school and often had extra English at lunch, but when they didn't, they were always willing to look for gold in the Yukon or try out new acts for the traveling circus, but Paige said she didn't like games and she especially didn't like anything "pretend."

But somehow when we'd meet at the tree, she didn't mind at all when I told her stories, which is weird, unless she thought they were history. She liked Apollo and Daphne, and Persephone being carried off to Hades, and Cupid falling in love with Psyche - stories my mother used to tell me and for some reason I have no trouble remembering at all.

In fact, Mr. C says I can remember perfectly well if I'm interested in something. But I think that must be true for everyone.

"It's too bad we don't have gods like that now," she sighed. "Our God is so boring."

I was a bit surprised but only because I didn't know her very well yet. "So, would you rather pray to Hermes? Or Mars maybe?"

"Of course. And we could ask Athena for help on our tests."

Not that she needed any help on her tests. "Yeah, or we could sing a hymn to Apollo for a sunny weekend."

"That's it! The main problem is that we don't have any magic in our lives."

Well, she didn't have any. That was for sure.

And then she got to the point. "Remember in the books we had when we were little how the kids would always get to wish for things?"

"And whatever they wished for always went wrong," I said. "It never worked out."

"That's because those kids were stupid. I'm not."

April 2nd: Paige may not be stupid, but she's pretty hard to play with.

CHAPTER THREE

I wanted to get her interested in a game I called *Runaway Children* which would have us hiding in an abandoned farmhouse, keeping pet squirrels, riding a stolen pony and foraging for food but of course that would count as "pretending."

So I kept going with the Greek myths. I'd climb up into the seat of the tree and say something like, "I am Juno, Queen of the Gods. Kneel when you approach my seat among the clouds!"

And she would check there weren't any twigs or stones or mud under her anywhere and then get down gingerly on one knee.

I went on. "You, Hermes, are to go among people with this golden scepter and wherever you hear a quarrel touch their shoulders and..."

"Wait. You don't mean really?

"Yes, really."

"You want me to go up to kids on the playground who are yelling or fighting each other and touch them on the shoulders with a stick?"

"Why not?"

"I think you should be Hermes. These are new jeans. I'll be Jupiter."

And so she'd be Jupiter but since she didn't want to act out anything where things actually happened she'd just sit there and maybe make a couple of long speeches and then it would be time for her to go home.

So I was trying to think of another game but the next time we got together it was raining so we went upstairs in my house.

She looked through all our box games and then asked me if we had a Ouija board. I said we didn't, but I'd done it once with my mother and nothing much happened. She said she had an aunt who had shown her how to do it but her mother wouldn't let her, but if my mother didn't mind then why didn't we do it here?

And then she surprised me by pulling an envelope out of her pocket. It was stuffed full of little papers cut out in small squares which had letters carefully drawn on them. And bigger ones with YES and NO and MAYBE.

And before I knew it, she was setting them all round the coffee table in our den as if it never occurred to her I might not want to do it with her.

I gave in and fetched a small glass from the washroom and then we sat down to try to contact someone dead. And after a moment of totally nothing, the glass did begin to move about slowly and nudged the YES and NO when we asked questions.

But it didn't spell out anything we could understand. Paige carefully wrote down each letter, but they didn't make any sense. We got something like: MXYLVRP.

"Maybe it's another language," she said, hopefully.

The glass kept on swinging back and forth in a seasick sort of way and in the end, we were getting so many words we couldn't read that I started pushing a little bit. But only to help it say something we could read.

It was really easy for some reason - even I could hardly tell I was doing it. I managed to spell "Greef" which was meant to be the start of "Greetings" only once I'd missed the "t" I couldn't really go back and fix it. Actually, I thought "Greef" would work pretty well as a message since it might be the beginning of something dramatic, but I was pretty sure it wasn't spelled that way.

And then I knew for sure it wasn't because Paige said, "Maybe it's a code." Her eyes were blue saucers. Then I started feeling guilty that she might notice I was pushing, so I said I wanted to stop and put it away.

"But I like it. Can we do it again next time?"

"We have lots of other games."

Her eyes flashed. "It is not a game. It's magic!"

Her thinking it was magic was the main reason I agreed to do it again the next day. I liked how much she wanted to believe it. She was so excited you could see a little vein in her neck pulsing.

"Is anybody there?" she asked as soon as we got our fingertips back on the glass.

I was starting to wonder why she didn't know there were movies and stories about kids getting in totally terrifying trouble doing this kind of thing. Even friendly spirits could cause problems if you carelessly set them free and left them hanging about. They might even try to possess you.

I was wanting to show that I wasn't that interested and was about to say we should quit, but just as I started to speak, I sort of shrugged and that sort of pushed down a bit on one side of the glass and it slipped and gave a little jump.

"Oh, there *is* someone there, isn't there?" she breathed.

Suddenly the tumbler was gliding around the table like it was on an ice rink. I knew I must be the one doing it because it wasn't her. My skin prickled.

"Would you tell us your name, please?" she pressed.

I couldn't really quit when it was so lively so I thought at least I could think up a name for the spirit. It needed to be something mystical and I'm not good at long words but I finally got the glass to spell out *Morgana*. I'm not sure if it's Irish but I've heard it before, and it sounded wise.

Paige was pretty sly though, because she immediately tried to test Morgana's supernatural insight. "Can you tell me my middle name?"

I didn't have a clue what her stupid middle name was and couldn't think of anything that even went well with *Paige* (Paige Amelia? Paige Rebecca?) so I thought I'd say something ridiculous and then finally she'd lose interest and we could stop.

"Thomas."

We looked at each other. "I don't think this is going anywhere," I said.

And I was just about to suggest we raid the kitchen when she said quietly, "My father's name is Thomas."

And then she stared at the glass intently. "Are you a very powerful spirit?"

I sighed, gave that a quick "YES" and waited. I didn't know where she was going next. I should have.

"I mean, for instance, can you grant wishes?"

I froze. The glass froze as well, and unluckily it was still right at the YES.

"Yes?" There was no stopping her now. "Yes, you can grant wishes?"

I slid the glass away from the YES, managed to nudge the MAYBE and quickly tried to get back in charge of the questions. But she barreled on.

"Can you see us right now?" That was an easy 'YES' and then, suddenly inspired, I chimed in, "If you know everything, can you see what Rory has in her pocket?"

Paige nodded her approval.

I carefully spelled out "rubber band" since I knew I had one and would be able to pull it out of my pocket right then, in triumph. Which I did.

"Isn't this wonderful?" Paige dropped her eyes in excited concentration and asked, "Could we ever see you?"

"No," said Morgana quickly. And then, to be sure, I had her add, "Never."

Paige wasn't as crushed as I had hoped and just went on calmly, "Do you know what we're going to have for dinner?" She was staying that night.

"Pasta" was right (and easy to spell) and I even managed to add, "And you have to go eat it now."

Then Morgana was gone.

"Aurora," Paige looked at me in wonder, "I think we're onto something."

Of course, Mr. C was at dinner with us that night. And, of course, he asked a lot about school because he went to some big university in California. He's an engineer, but not the train kind. Anyway, he was impressed with Paige. She got straight "A's" at her last school and was able to tell him the main rivers and lakes in any country he asked about (and he asked about quite a few.)

But then he suddenly asked what Paige was using the audio recorder for. The one I said I lent her. She looked so blank I had to say, "No, it wasn't Paige, Mr. Cullen, sorry, it was Abbey."

They all stared at me, Mum too, but no one said any more about it.

April 7th: I wish some of Paige's brains would rub off on me.

CHAPTER FOUR

It wasn't my fault that Paige got carried away so quickly. It was her fault, too.

We were in school and having a special art class. We don't have regular ones and of course there is no special art teacher, but Ms. Patel lets us have an hour or so a month as a treat because she really likes art.

And that day she asked us to all think of our favorite animal and draw that.

My mother once gave me a whole set of colored pencils which I keep under my bed. I'm afraid to use them because chances are they will start to get lost and then Mum will be disappointed. Paige has a fancier set made somewhere in Europe and she lets me use them if we're together because of course she puts each one back in its correct slot right away.

I drew a horse. I'm not a brilliant artist but I can make a horse look pretty much like a horse and I like flicking the pencil between the ears to make the mane. I drew this one standing in some grass so you couldn't really see its hooves or the bulgy ankle bits right above the hooves because they're quite hard to draw.

Anyway, Ms. Patel looked over my shoulder and smiled and said, "That's lovely, Rory. Really nice."

And suddenly Paige piped up and said, "Rory has one like that in her bedroom she did a while ago. It's even better than that one."

I tried to make my eyebrows say '*What?!*' to Paige, but by then Ms. Patel was interested and of course she was still making a special fuss of whatever Paige said because she was so new. She turned to me.

"Would you like to bring it in to show everyone, Rory?"

Paige was grinning. "Of course she will. And I have an idea. What if she brings it in and we have a contest to name the pony? And give a prize to the winner. Or maybe the picture could be the prize!"

Ms. Patel looked surprised, and she wasn't the only one. Paige might as well have grabbed my hand and jumped off a cliff taking me with her.

"What do you think, Rory? A contest is always fun. Although you don't have to give the picture away if you don't want to."

"I..."

"Well, you don't have to decide now. But do bring the picture in on Monday. Now we've heard about it, we'd all be thrilled to see it, wouldn't we, class?"

Some of the students murmured vaguely without looking up from their work.

Half an hour later on the playground I grabbed hold of Paige's coat sleeve, fuming. "I don't have another picture in my room! You know that, right? I get into enough trouble at school without you..."

"You won't get into trouble," replied Paige smoothly. "If you bring in the picture."

"How? I have to draw another picture over the weekend?"

"No."

"Then where am I supposed to get it?"

"We're going to wish for it."

I don't know how long I stared at her before she smirked and said, "What's wrong? Don't worry. We can do it Sunday."

"Do what?" I croaked.

"Wish for it. See you then."

April 9th: Paige is getting really pushy.

CHAPTER FIVE

My father used to say I had Buddha Ears. I don't remember him very well, but I do remember that. He probably meant they're big, which they are, but I like to think he also meant I could hear very well. Which I can.

But sometimes when we're driving in the car my mother will say things like, "Just look at the color of those maples!" And I will look around, though by then we've passed them so she frowns, "Why don't you answer, darling? Didn't you hear me?" And of course I did, but I'm thinking, too. I think this means it takes me too long to think.

I can also look right at someone when they're talking and not hear a word they say. But when I'm not thinking of something else, I can hear really well.

That night mother was talking to Mr. C. (I'm supposed to call him Doug but at least I've stopped calling him Mr. Cullen.

I can just about manage 'Mr. C'.) I had just stopped on my way to the closet in the front hall because I knew there was a sheet of white cardboard there.

He said:	She holds a pen with her whole fist. Of course, her handwriting is terrible.
She said:	That's not so very serious, Doug.
He said:	She needs help. With everything. You've got to get her a tutor.
She said:	I think she needs more time away from school, not more of it.
He said:	I think she needs to try harder, Katie.

My mother didn't say anything else. After he had gone, I laid the cardboard on the dining room table with my full set of perfectly sharpened pencils.

She smiled. "What are you going to draw?"

"A horse. It's a contest. I might need some help."

"I can't help you if it's a contest, darling."

"Oh no, sorry, it's not a contest. It's not. Just an assignment. Please?"

I started the outline of a hill. I looked at my hand and sure enough I was holding the pencil with my whole fist. But I did sketch out a plump gray pony with his dark mane and tail whipped by the wind. The shape was good. His ears were good. Mum only had to help me with the shading. And the coloring. And the eyes.

I forgot to put the pencils back, but Mum must have cleared up because they were all organized with the lid back on and on the carpet outside my door when I came to bed tonight.

April 10th: My handwriting IS terrible. And I do hold my pencil wrong.

CHAPTER SIX

And on Sunday she came.

"Rory!" called my mother. "Paige's here."

But as soon as we were in my room, I turned on her. "I'm warning you, if this doesn't work you're going to get up in front of the whole class and tell everyone you lied."

She finally looked alarmed. "But you believe it will work, don't you? It will work."

I shrugged. We set up the letters and I was thinking this wasn't a nice thing to do, even to Paige.

"Can we speak to Morgana?" I asked the glass.

"But don't sound angry," begged Paige. "We have to ask a huge favor." And then, using her most polite voice, "May we please talk to you?"

"Well?" came the reply.

"There's something we'd like to ask for," said Paige.

No reply. Just slow circling. Like a hawk.

"You know the picture that Rory did in class on Friday?"

"Yes."

"Would it be possible to make another one...I mean make a whole new one appear? Only maybe bigger?"

Silence. Then, "What will you do for me?"

This didn't stop her. I guess I didn't expect it to. "What could we do?"

"Serve me." I don't know why I said that, but I liked it when she went even paler.

"Right now?" she blinked.

"I will let you know."

"And the picture?" I asked.

"Behind the sofa. Paige must reach down and touch it first. That will make it appear." Then the glass went still. My fingers ached.

"Well, go on, then," I said, sharply. "Go look!"

Paige pushed her bangs from her eyes, knelt up on the couch, and, pressing her cheek against the wallpaper, reached down.

"There's something there!" Her fingers closed on the cardboard and she inched it up, then flung it, almost in horror, onto the carpet.

I stepped forward as she hopped down and we both stood gazing at a drawing of the plump pony with a dark shaggy mane, alone on a snowy hill.

"Oh, Rory," she cried. "It's *so* much better than yours!"

April 11th: Sometimes it's really hard to like Paige.

CHAPTER SEVEN

"Has anyone seen it yet?" asked Paige, lacing up her indoor shoes. Mine have Velcro because I'm very slow with laces. Mr. Cullen tried to teach me another way where you do something with two loops he called butterflies, but it wasn't any easier.

"Let's hurry. I can't wait." She stopped in the corridor and looked at me and whispered, "but what do you suppose she'll want us to do?"

"Ms. Patel?"

"No, dummy. Morgana! She said she wants us to serve her."

"No idea," I said. That was true.

Ms. Patel liked the picture and liked that I was happy for it to be given as a prize to the person who thought up the best name. I couldn't wait to get rid of it.

She took a shoebox and marked it "Pony Naming Contest" and put folded paper ballots next to it. At the end of the week, she said she would read out all the suggestions and we'd vote on the best name and then the picture would be awarded.

My mother once told me that most children ask 'why?' about everything when they're about three years old and that she was surprised that I never asked 'why?' about anything. Ever. Then she would nudge me and say that was because I was 'away with faeries,' happy as a little elf. I want to think that was a good thing, but I'm pretty sure it wasn't.

It doesn't do you much good at school, that's for sure. But since I brought in the pony picture no one has rolled their eyes at my mistakes as much, not even when I said I didn't know where the sun sets. I was about to say, 'behind The No Frills Food Barn', but I stopped myself just in time. I know what I was supposed to say now. It's the West.

Ronnie even asked me if I'd taken art lessons after school somewhere. And Phyllis gave me some Maltesers at lunch. And Carl held the library door open almost long enough for me to go through after him.

But all Paige kept asking was how we were going to serve Morgana so we could get another wish.

I have a lot of ideas about lots of things, which would be good if I knew how to make them happen. Usually, they go wrong and I end up wishing I hadn't even tried.

I was getting pretty anxious to stop this game from getting out of hand – any more than it already had. So, I tore off a piece of paper and wrote a short note in pencil. And I made the letters very curvy, so it didn't look like I had done it. Then I found Paige's coat in our hall and slipped it into her pocket.

Of course, the next day Paige was bouncing up and down like a basketball. "I'm telling you I found it in my coat pocket when I got home last night! Look at it, the handwriting's all wavy, I'm sure it's from Morgana...see? It's signed, see? With an "M."

I took the folded square from her and pretended to be disappointed, "It doesn't look very magical. It's on pretty ordinary paper."

"Never mind that. Just read it."

I unfolded the paper and looked at the long, snaky letters: "Do not ask me again for help. I can only help relatives and loved ones. M." I was pretty pleased with it and pretty sure Paige's interest would start dribbling away now for sure.

It didn't.

"Okay. So we have to think of a reason for her to help us."

"Like... what?"

"I've got it, I've got it, I know, I know!" She whipped her hat up in the air and was so busy clapping she forgot to catch it and it landed in a puddle.

"What?"

"We'll ask who her relatives are, whoever's still alive, you know, then we can write to them, or deliver a message, and then bring messages back to her. We could even do them favors like cutting their lawn or putting seeds in their birdfeeders, if they live nearby."

I didn't know what to say. I think my mouth was open during her whole speech.

"Well," I managed finally, "I don't know. I guess we could ask her."

When we sat down to summon Morgana again, I quickly spelled out, "Yes, I am here." Maybe a bit too quickly because Paige said, "It seems to go faster when I only have one hand on. Maybe you should only use one hand, too."

I left both hands on, but took the hint to cut back on the speed as I made M add, "What do you want now?"

Paige was eager. "We were hoping that there was someone, a friend, or relative we could contact for you."

Morgana considered this for a while, circling, then very slowly spelled out "Albert Cordelli."

"But we know him," said Paige, flustered. He was the combination Phys Ed and science teacher at Franklin Park and I had seen his name written down on a card next to his door, so I knew how to spell it.

"Give him a matchbox with a rusty nail inside. He will understand."

I have no idea why I came up with that. Then Morgana went on to tell us that we must not contact any other spirits, and after we did the task she set for us, then *maybe* she would grant us a wish.

All of this took me a good five minutes, but Paige was almost drooling. "How will it work? When we wish? Can we be anywhere? Do we have to close our eyes?"

I slowed the glass. My head ached from all the concentrating and spelling.

"Are you going?" asked Paige. "Don't go!"

I removed my hands. "I'm not sure we should give Mr. Cordelli a message like that."

"If we leave it on his desk, he wouldn't see us. He's always in the gym before class."

"She said she couldn't promise it would work."

"It will. I just know it."

April 13th: I really wish I knew how to stop this Game.

CHAPTER EIGHT

My mother says I need to do chores to earn an allowance and she's trying me out with the dusting. I was doing the vacuuming for a while but I bumped it into the edges of the walls and sometimes that chipped the paint on the baseboards. The dusting is better. There's the lemon smell of the polish and there's also my mother's dresser. She has a carved wooden jewelry box and a crystal tray with a hairbrush and mirror with matching gold handles. On top of the jewelry box she keeps a cameo brooch my father gave her. It's a woman's head with curly hair and it does look like her.

I was in my room trying to find my plaid shirt when my mother came in. She won't let me keep my door closed and that means I don't have much time to prepare if I think she's going to be annoyed.

"Rory, have you seen my cameo?" she asked, not adding "darling" or anything to let me know she wasn't upset. And when she is upset that means she is going to get more upset the more we talk.

"No." That wasn't really true. I had seen it on Saturday morning when I was dusting, but I knew she meant had I seen it today, and I hadn't.

She sighed and looked around, then went straight to the white headboard behind my bed. And there it was, right next to the base of the lamp. She held it up. "What's this?"

"Sorry."

"You know I don't like you just borrowing things like that."

"I didn't mean to." This was true. I must have been looking at it and walked out of her room not knowing it was in my hand. I didn't mean to bring it in my room.

"And I don't like you taking anything without asking me first."

"I know."

"What were you doing with it?"

"Nothing."

"It's mine, you know that."

Now, as I say, when my mother gets going on a subject she's upset about, she can go on about it for a long time.

"I didn't mean to take it."

"You can't take something accidentally."

"But I don't remember taking it."

"How could you not remember taking it?"

It was hard to believe for me, too, but it was true. "I'm sorry."

"It's not something to play with."

"I know."

"Please don't take it again."

"I won't."

She was quiet a moment, but breathing a bit strangely. Then she finally turned and left. There was a smeary bit of dust where she'd moved the lamp so I rubbed it with the sleeve of my plaid shirt. At least I had found that.

At school it was little Abbey Benson who won the pony picture, after the class all voted that the name they liked best was hers: *Sweetbriar*. She seemed really happy with the drawing, and her hair, which is long and dark, looks a lot like the pony's mane, so that was good, too.

Then Ms. Patel handed out a glossy magazine with pictures of chocolate bars and a money envelope and told us all we needed to sell a lot of candy, or get our parents and relatives to sell a lot of candy, to raise money for the May Fair and whoever sold the most would win a prize. Maybe she could have saved the pony picture for that. She never said what this new prize would be.

That night I had to draw a map of Canada with all the provinces and label all the mountains and prairies and capitals and Mum got the pencils out again and helped.

Then she went through my backpack like she does every night so she doesn't miss any hand-outs, assignments or messages from the school, or forms she has to sign, and she pulled out the chocolate fundraising booklet.

"I hate these things," she said. "But I suppose I can buy a few and give them out at work." She works at a doctor's office, making appointments and welcoming the patients as they come in. She laid out the order form and quickly checked off a few boxes and said I should get ready for bed.

Mum used to read me legends about changelings and selkies, but now I'm older she says I need to read things for myself. And I do. In fact, sometimes I read a book more than once because it's easier the second time.

Of course Paige is better at everything at school than me, But then so are Carl and Phyllis. And little Abbey. So are the twins next door. Even Jasmine and Mikayla are better than me and English isn't even their first language.

And my mother, she can do anything. I wish I was seven again. Or six. I think Daddy was still here then.

April 20th: I miss being read to.

CHAPTER NINE

My mother says we need to work more on a routine because a good routine frees you up to think of more important things. And that takes the pressure off. But I think it puts pressure on. When I have to clear the table (every other night) or put the dishes away (every *other* other night) I sometimes say I don't feel well although then Mr. C frowns and says that's funny because I felt well enough to eat.

So sometimes I have to go and make myself throw up just to make him feel bad, which he does. At least then I can lie down and not have to remember where to put things or be told I'm too slow. I don't drop things though. I don't do that.

Last night Mr. C said that I should have been born left-handed because that would have gone better with the way my brain works. I didn't mind him saying that too much considering he usually acts like he doesn't think my brain works at all.

Anyway, it worked well enough to find a rusty nail in a jar in the garage. And to remember that my father used to smoke a pipe. I found a box which had a few wooden matches left and we dumped them out and put the rusty nail in that.

And leaving it on Mr. Cordelli's desk before school was just as easy as we thought it would be. He was in the gym using a pump to put more air into the balls and I watched the door to the corridor as Paige darted into his classroom and put it next to a pile of pens. I was hoping he'd never even notice it and then Morgana could say it hadn't worked and tell us we should just leave her alone.

"Maybe Morgana's full name is Morgana Cordelli," Paige said as we shivered on the playground at recess. Her coat was open at the neck and I saw she was wearing a small gold chain with a blue stone on it.

"It's a sapphire. It's my birthstone. My father sent it to me."

"He sent it?" I couldn't remember her saying anything about her father before.

"He's in hospital."

"Oh."

"I wear it every day. You never notice anything, do you?" She paused and narrowed her eyes. "Where's your father, anyway?"

"Well, see, he was a writer…"

"He wrote books?"

"No, more for newspapers and…"

"A journalist?"

"Yes. But...he knew too much."

"You don't mean..." her eyes widened again. "He's in prison?"

"No. No. He died."

"You don't mean somebody killed him?"

"I don't know. No one knows." I wanted to make it mysterious. The truth was that my father was also in hospital before he died. For a pretty long time, I think. But I didn't say that. People don't always die in hospitals, and I didn't want her to think hers would.

And Paige was really, really nice to me for the rest of the day.

But the next day Mr. Cordelli was absent, and someone said that when he left after school he seemed upset. Like he'd had bad news.

But Paige said that was wonderful because it must mean he understood the message and that meant we'd done it right and that now we could have our first wish. I thought we should report to Morgana first but Paige said she already knew what the wish should be and she wanted to try it out on Saturday at her house where we couldn't do the board anyway and that there was no point in telling Morgana first as she would already know all about it since she was magic, so it must be all right. I was still worried about Mr. Cordelli.

So, on the weekend I went to Paige's where her mother never asks us to clear up after lunch. We went up to her room leaving all the plates on the table. "Can we talk about this?"

"It's a good wish."

"What if it doesn't work?"

"What if it does?"

Her room is a chilly pink with a carpet the color of popcorn. We sat on the bed. She was gazing at the shelf above her dresser where there is a small herd of chubby white china horses. As soon as she sat down, she scrunched up her face and announced, "I wish my horses would come to life!"

I swallowed. Here was the moment of truth and I had no plan. We both looked at the horses.

A full minute passed. Nothing happened.

"Maybe we have to say it with our eyes closed?"

"That's stupid. We couldn't see them, then."

"I mean, maybe we should say the wish with our eyes closed and then open them." I was hoping that when they didn't start prancing about, I could blame it on the exact words or order of words we'd used when we wished. "Or maybe we have to say it three times, or..."

"Let's try saying it together."

"I really think we ought to wait and ask..."

"No!"

So we stared right at the horses and she said slowly, "I wish that my horses would come to life." I tried to say it with her, but it came out as a kind of echo. "You're too slow. Anyway, they're not your horses," she hissed. "You can't say *my*...Oh, why don't we just say *the china horses on the shelf?*"

So we tried again, slowly, "We wish that the china horses on the shelf would come to life."

And then Paige thought we ought to add "in Paige's room" so we did that as well.

At this point we'd been staring at them for so long I was pop-eyed. I was willing them to move so desperately my head was swimming with the strain. Another minute. My mother says that in ancient religions you could make any object holy simply by believing it was. So for instance if you worshipped a perfectly ordinary stone long enough it would actually start to glow. If this was even the tiniest bit true we had a chance. But after another minute I was aching to give up. But just as I began to let my eyes close there was a low croon from Paige.

"Oh. They're moving."

I tried hard to focus and couldn't - or was there a slight movement in the blur? It almost looked like a breeze might be tossing a tiny mane.

Paige was swaying a little. "They are. They're moving." A smile played on her face.

I blinked and rubbed the skin around my eyes with one hand and drew it away again.

No. They weren't moving. Well, the whole group wasn't. But wasn't that a tail switching? There. A little hoof pawing the ground? I held my breath, trying not to blink. Every time my eyes passed from one to the other, I thought maybe I had just missed some really big movement and the animals were cleverly, slyly, trying to hide their real and secret freedom.

"They're moving. They are, they are," chanted Paige.

There? That might have been an ear flicking. I couldn't tell what I was seeing any more.

"Just look, oh look," Paige was still murmuring, and I was starting to feel faint when the bedroom door was nudged open and Mrs. Worthing entered, a tray in her hands. "Hello, hello!" she smiled warmly. "What are you two mice up to? I brought you some ice cream up as a treat."

Her mother set the tray down on the desk and glanced at Paige who was staring at her, furious. "Now those aren't tears, are they, Paige?"

"No, Mum. We were playing a game of concentration." But her eyes were brimming.

"Well, I'm sorry to interrupt. I'll run along now. Don't let the ice cream melt." She closed the door and was gone.

Suddenly Paige was in a flat-out rage. "She did it on purpose. She's always ruining things. Bitch. Bitch. Bitch!" Hot tears were coming fast and she was making choking sounds.

"Don't! Please don't cry, please, she couldn't have known we were doing anything important..."

"Oh, never mind," she sniffed, grabbing a handful of tissues from a box by her bed. "It doesn't matter. It doesn't matter." She snuffled and swallowed and blew her nose and looked up at me glumly. "Well, don't just sit there. Go ahead. Eat your ice cream."

April 28th: Paige scares me sometimes.

CHAPTER TEN

My mother says where other people have thoughts, I have emotions. But Paige is in a class by herself.

I spent Sunday morning trying to think of a way to refuse to contact Morgana again. Or for her to refuse to contact us. And then to make her disappear for good.

But Paige was so low and gloomy when she came over, I felt sorry for her. She said the only good thing that had happened all year was having that wish about the horses work. Or almost work. And the next one would be even better, wouldn't it? Or did I think that Morgana was angry with us?

I knew she was going to want to go straight upstairs and set up the board and I just couldn't face it, so I announced that I really, really wanted some red licorice and could we run up to the small row of stores on the main street? They were just a few blocks from my house. Paige shrugged glumly and came. She liked crosswords and quizzes, so she ended up buying a magazine. Then she said she really wanted this particular gel pen with a silver star pattern and purple ink she'd seen there once, but we looked everywhere and couldn't find it. But then, just as we were leaving, sure enough, I spotted a cardboard box next to the far counter with a pile of multi-colored gel pens and I suddenly thought that if we did make just one more wish, one that I could actually make work, then maybe I could make her happy.

And then we could quit. For good. For one thing it was getting much too hard spelling out answers to everything. I already had to explain that Morgana's spelling wasn't too good because she was a poor Irish girl who had died young and hadn't had much schooling.

As we cut back through the woods to come up the back slope to my house, I was chewing fast to get rid of the red licorice since of course I wasn't allowed it, so we decided to stop at the Gods and Goddesses tree.

Paige leaned against it but when I climbed up to the hollow, she scowled up at me. "Hurry up and finish that stuff or hide it or something. We have to ask Morgana if she's happy with us now."

I think it was the scowl that did it. I stared off in the distance thinking, and before I even meant to, I answered in a trance-like tone. "I'm not unhappy with you."

She leaped to her feet and stared up at me. "Morgana?"

"It is." I had no trouble with the soft Irish accent since my mother still had more than a bit of one even though she'd come over with my dad years and years ago, before I was born.

"Where's Rory?" Paige was looking more thrilled than puzzled.

"She is safe. I am just borrowing her sweet self for a bit."

"Thank you for the wish!" Paige chirped up politely.

"Oh, you're welcome." I was trying to make my gaze both hypnotic and friendly, but the truth was she was too entranced to care. "Albert got his message and I'm grateful for that."

"Is there anything else we can do for you?"

"I am in need of a wee rest today."

"Oh, don't go!"

"But you can come here to the tree when you want to speak to me."

"But couldn't we help do something else for someone, somewhere? So we could have one more wish?"

I was prepared for this. But I didn't want to deliver any more messages and risk upsetting more people. "I believe that Rory's mother would be very grateful for some help with the dishes today."

"I can do that! I mean, we can. Yes. For sure."

"After that you can decide on your wish," I lifted my hand in a kind of general blessing and let my head fall forward and come up again with what I hoped was a stunned expression.

"Paige? What happened? I feel funny."

"She was here! Rory, she was here, I swear. In person. You should have heard her!"

"I think...I sort of did. In my head." I figured this would save her having to repeat everything back to me. "Didn't she say we could have another wish?"

"Yes, isn't that great? But what? Oh, let's not waste it. We should wish for something really good."

"But not too big. We shouldn't seem greedy. Hey, remember what you were saying today, about that gel pen you wanted?"

"Uh. Yes. But..."

"I'd like to have one, too. Why don't we wish for one each?"

"But they're not there anymore."

"They don't have to be. We're getting them by magic."

She nodded slowly. "Oh. Yes. Okay. Perfect."

And so, Paige, who had probably never washed a dish in her life, spent fifteen minutes hard at it after my mother's homemade macaroni and cheese that lunchtime and even suggested we go back and scrub the pan we left soaking in hot soapy water for half an hour. Mum let us watch some shorts on YouTube while it soaked. Animal ones. And when I used her tea towel with the Irish Whiskey recipe on it to mop up the splashes on the floor, she didn't even flinch. She just smiled at me.

April 29th: Today was fun.

CHAPTER ELEVEN

When Mr. C heard we were having a May Fair at Franklin Park he suggested we bring back some old-time playground games like hopscotch and Dutch skipping and marbles. And he thought it would be great (and very good practice for me) if I was the one who organized this.

So, he sent me to school with his printed-out list of old-fashioned fun for me to give to Ms. Patel. I kept it in my hand and didn't put it in my backpack so I wouldn't forget. I think he wanted me to set up an after-school planning meeting as well, but I was hoping maybe Ms. Patel would do all that and handing it in to her would be enough.

One of the indoor games we could do in the gym if the weather wasn't great was called *Fan the Fish* and another was called *Lemon Golf* and he said they were both fun and he had played them with his family long before everybody had all these screens and devices and endless online distractions and stuff.

And then he decided to show me. My mother looked happy that Mr. C was going to play with me and even happier that I was going to play with him.

So we cut out two fish-shaped pieces of stiff paper and put one on the floor in front of each of us. Then we stood side-by-side holding folded newspapers and began fanning the fish like mad to try to get them to lift up and tumble forward toward the finish line.

Before I knew it, I was laughing with him as my fish curled up and somersaulted backwards or suddenly shot up in the air and scooted further forward. He won. And he hadn't tried to let me win which I was pleased about.

But then we tried the other one.

He found two umbrellas with curved handles and we had to hold them upside down like golf clubs while we carefully lined up our shot and hit a lemon to make it roll toward a goal line. The winner would be whoever got it there first.

Lemons aren't round so of course they wobble away in surprising directions and it's funny when they suddenly decide to end up behind the couch.

He chuckled as he fished his out from under the coffee table. "Frustrating, isn't it? They trick you, because they start out perfectly well. Sorta like you, Rory."

I blinked.

"I mean we can give you a nudge in the right direction, but you never do what anyone expects. And that's not a bad thing. Always."

"I have to go to the washroom, Mr. C."

And still grinning he called after me, "Hey, Rory, isn't it time you called me Doug?"

The next day Paige was absent. I called her when I got home to see how she was and she sounded tired but she asked me to come over and tell her what happened at school.

"I bet I didn't miss anything important," she said when she opened the door. I didn't know if she had because I didn't know what she would think was important. And I hadn't thought to pick up any assignments. I told her we played dodgeball at lunch.

Her mother didn't seem to be around. Paige said she was out buying stuff to decorate the kitchen which was good because she wanted to show me something in the greenhouse. So we went out round the back and pushed open the sagging wooden door.

"Do you know what these are?" she asked, pointing to a row of small brown pots on an old bench.

"Plants?" I was trying to make her smile, which was always hard.

"Herbs."

"Right. For cooking."

"Duh. But you know what these are?"

"Mushrooms." There was a whole tray of them under the bench, pushing out of the crumbling soil with their pale grubby caps and dark undersides. I don't like eating them so we never have them at home.

"My mother grows them."

"I can see that."

"And my father is sick in hospital."

"Yes. Oh. Wait. You don't think…?"

"It would have been easy for her, wouldn't it?"

"Why would she…?""

"She doesn't like him."

"Paige…"

"Oh, I knew you wouldn't believe me. No one ever believes me!" She burst into tears, took off back into the house, and slammed the door shut behind her. She must have gone upstairs because I knocked but she never let me back in.

That was Thursday and since she was so upset I wanted to buy the pens more than ever. Then I could have them magically appear somewhere she wouldn't expect. The trouble was I didn't have enough money. I didn't get my allowance until Sunday and Saturday was when I would see Paige, so I thought maybe I could borrow just a little.

But my mother and Mr. C were having coffee in the living room and I didn't want to ask for money in front of him. Especially after the game of Lemon Golf which nobody won because I never came back to finish it and that's just the sort of thing he doesn't like.

He said:	She doesn't finish anything. She daydreams.
She said:	Her father was a dreamer, too. He was. We have to give her time.
He said:	Then you need to stop helping her so much. There's a word for that.

I didn't wait to hear what the word was. The trouble with Mum's confidence in me is that it mostly just makes me more afraid I'll fail.

My mother's purse is always on her bedside table or on the floor next to it. I was pretty sure the pens wouldn't be much more than two dollars each. But when I looked in her wallet the smallest bill was a ten. But then I realized it might be okay. First, I would put back the change, and then as soon as I got my allowance I could put back whatever the pens cost. So it would add back up. And she might not notice.

After school I walked up to the drug store and passed Abbey running up and down her driveway, flinging her head from side to side and sending her long hair flying back and forth like a great dark flag, flapping on her neck and shoulders. She stopped when she saw me and tried to smile.

"What are you playing?"

"Nothing. I hafta get my haircut. I just wanted to feel it for a while more."

"Why are you getting it cut?"

"Tanya. And the others."

"What about them?" Abbey whispered, "They held me down so my hair all fell into the toilet, and they started dunking it and wiping it round the bowl. I tried to wash it out when I got home, but my mother came in and...and I guess it still stank."

Her eyes were filling up then, so I reached out and squeezed her hand, but just at that moment a car went by and two girls leaned out the back window, laughing, and Abbey turned and ran into the house.

When I got to the store the box of gel pens was still in the same place. There weren't too many which had purple ink, though, and hardly any that were the same. And only one of them had silver stars. There was a matching pair of pens that had a swirly, pink pearl finish but that wasn't what she'd asked for.

So, I could get two the same or I could get the pink pearl for me and the one with stars for her. It took me a long time to decide but I chose the two different ones in the end, so she really could, just this once, get exactly what she wished for.

That night my mother had a headache. She was lying in the dark in her bedroom after dinner and she called to me that she couldn't find an aspirin in her purse and asked if I could get the bottle from the bathroom shelf.

I opened the mirror cabinet and looked at the jumbled row of Band-Aids and mouthwash and eyedrops and tried to read all the plastic bottles but I didn't know what the color or the size of the aspirin bottle would be so I had to go back to her bedroom and say I couldn't find it.

She sighed and checked her purse again, then finally got up and lurched to the bathroom and came back with the bottle herself.

She looked at me, baffled. "It was right there," she said, holding it up.

"I didn't see it. I'm sorry. I couldn't..." My throat was closing up and my voice was disappearing.

"No, never mind. Doesn't matter. But it's almost empty. I'll drop by the drug store tomorrow and..."

Then she stopped. Suddenly her wallet was open and she was frowning. "I'm missing a ten. You didn't take anything out of my purse, did you, Rory?"

"No." I shook my head, and my heart was beating fast. I wanted to say I took it, but I froze. And I'd forgotten to put the change back and it was too late now. And even if I put my allowance back in on Sunday, she would notice that she had more than she should have because she'd just counted it.

"I did buy milk today, but I thought..." And she collapsed back on the bed. "Oh hell. Would you get me a glass of water, darling?"

I did that right away. And I found a washcloth and ran cold water on it and folded it up and put it gently on her forehead and she said 'thank you' but she didn't smile.

May 4th: Now everyone is disappointed in me.

CHAPTER TWELVE

On Saturday morning Mum was still looking like she wanted to say something but kept changing her mind, so I thought I would do the dusting early and maybe that would make her happier and that's when I found what I found in the bookshelf.

It was a notebook with an old black speckled cardboard cover and quite a few loose pages, some of them just starting to turn tea-colored around the edges.

Inside it said "For R." and I wondered if that meant me.

When I told Paige that my father wrote for the newspapers, that part was true. And Mum said that he wrote other things as well. So, it seemed like this was something important. There were lots of lines started and then scratched out again. One that was left was: "*She washed the house until it smelled of apples.*"

Well, that wasn't about me.

Then on the next page there was a poem:

I clasped a slender tree
and a nymph bloomed there
like a blossom in the boughs.
Will she tumble down to me?

Which could have been about me, I guess. But probably not. Then suddenly there was a voice behind me and I jumped a mile.

"I was going to show you."
"What?"
"Your Dad's notebook. I keep forgetting."
"You never forget anything. It's me who forgets."
"And your Daddy. He forgot things."
"What did he forget?"
"He forgot...to stay with us." She reached down to take the notebook, her eyes misting and her voice tight. But she swallowed and started to read with not much expression at all.

"Other children's dolls are trimmed with lace.
But your dolls are in tatters because they have adventures."
"That one was for me!"
"I was always thinking I might have the book printed up and give it to you. On your sixteenth birthday maybe. But then why? It's not even finished. It's just notes. He never really finished anything. Except life. He finished that."

"He didn't finish it..." I couldn't say the words "on purpose" but she was already answering me.

"No, no, it was the pipe. I told you. I think he just wanted to look like a writer. And he did, too. For a while. But it wasn't good for him. It made him ill."

I wanted to ask how exactly it had made him ill, but then I had the feeling that I'd already been told a long time ago, and I didn't want her to think I didn't remember something that important.

I still wanted to ask if the notebook was mine or not but she was already reading something else, this time to herself. And then she was brushing her cheeks quickly and turning away and taking the notebook with her.

I don't even know where it is now.

There are two things about our next-door neighbors which are interesting.

On one side of us are the twins, Stephen and Stuart, who are a year older than me and go to a private school.

When we were much younger, they asked me to come under their back porch with them so we could take off our pants and stick long stalks of meadow grass up our bums. I said 'no' but they made me stay and watch them anyway. I haven't played with them since.

The only reason they are interesting now is that they always wave before they get into the car in the morning to be driven to wherever their school is. And they look like kids who go to Hogwarts with their scarves and school uniforms, especially when it's snowing and their identical ears and noses are raw and red.

The second thing (unless you count the twins as two things) is that there is a beehive in the garden of the house on the other side of us. This belongs to Mrs. Harvey who wears a bulky bright yellow suit and a hood with mesh on the face when she goes down to see them. Sometimes I slip under the fence and stand to one side to watch the bees hurrying in and out the tray at the bottom.

Last Christmas she gave my mother a jar of honey with a handwritten label, and it tasted of last spring and next spring rolled into one.

I wanted to be by myself after finding my father's notebook, and before Paige came over, so I sat down near the bees. But just then Mrs. Harvey came out, in her daffodil-colored coveralls from head to toe. I'm pretty sure she smiled at me but of course I couldn't see her face. She never minds me coming over.

"Hello, Rory. You need to stand back today. I'm going to disturb them a bit." She pointed to the long wooden strip with its rows of small holes over the bottom tray of the hive.

"I put a mouse guard on the entrance last fall," she said as I moved behind her. "So that they don't get in over the winter when the bees are sleeping."

I wondered if mice ate honey, but I didn't ask because people usually tell me a lot more details than I can manage at once. And I knew Mrs. Harvey would be happy to go on for quite a while. And she did.

"Mice love honey as much as we do and of course it's a nice, dark, warm place for them," she said. "And sometimes a mouse can live in a hive for quite a while before the bees notice it's there."

I was trembling a bit. I didn't really want her to go on. But she did.

"Of course, when they do discover it, the bees will sting it to death."

She gave me the screws to hold as she undid the mouse guard. While she was taking it off three bees came and landed on my sleeve.

Mrs. Harvey turned and caught her breath and said, "Don't move. Those are workers. They can sting."

I stood very still and they walked up and down for a bit and then went back to the hive. She nodded, and probably looked pleased although I couldn't see for sure because she still had the cage thing on her head.

"Some people never seem to get stung," she said. "Perhaps it's their smell. What are they called? Pheromones or hormones or something."

I didn't think it would be hormones in my case as I'm pretty sure I don't have any yet.

"Did you know there's an old tradition that if someone in the house dies or is born or gets married you must *tell the bees*? Maybe even put a white ribbon, or a black one, on the hive. And if you don't..." She was packing up her tools. "They say the bees may all fly away. Find somewhere else, where they feel valued. Where they're part of the family."

Just then I heard Paige's voice calling. She sounded excited so I crunched out of the Harveys' gravel driveway and met her on the curb.

"Where shall we go?" She was rubbing her raw hands.

"If you're cold we could sit in the car." Mum hadn't been out since she came home from work yesterday and she never locked the car.

I slipped in behind the steering wheel and Paige sat next to me in front of the glove compartment. It took us a while to get the words right. But finally, we chanted together: "We wish for two gel pens with purple ink!" I had to convince her not to get fussy about the color of the pens themselves.

Paige opened her eyes and looked in her lap. "Nothing here."

"Me neither," I tried to sound disappointed. "Do you want to check the pocket in your door?" I pretended to look down and check mine, but it had given Paige the idea. She flipped open the glove compartment and gasped in delight. There, side by side, were two pens – one pearl pink and the other white with silver stars. Paige seized them.

"Which one do you want?" she cried even though she had asked for one with stars. "I want this one!" She didn't wait for me to answer and held up the pink pearl one triumphantly. So I got the one with the stars. Which was fine.

And then she fell to scribbling happily all over the cover of a local street map, thrilled at the sparkly shade of purple.

After that we had some cocoa and Paige had to go home and I asked my mother for help with a page of spelling words but she was pretty quiet while we did it.

May 5th: A mouse shouldn't try to live in a beehive.

CHAPTER THIRTEEN

In my dream I was standing in a meadow watching a small shaggy black bull charging round and round. He came pretty close to me on one clattering sweep, but I kept very still and he wheeled away.

Suddenly he trotted to a stop and his legs began going back and forth like scissors in a comical, stiff-legged bouncy dance. He scooped up a sweatshirt I guess I had dropped (even though it was blue, not red like they normally like) and began tossing it around on his horns. He was trying to look fierce, but you could tell he was enjoying himself. Then suddenly a pickup truck crashed through the farm fence full of men with rifles all firing at him while I yelled, "No, Stop! He was dancing! He was only playing!"

"Rory," said my mother, shaking me gently. "It's seven-thirty."

"What time is it?" I managed.

"I just told you, it's... Never mind. It's time to get up. I'm toasting a bagel for you." She stopped at the door and looked back. "Are you okay?"

I stared up at the dreamcatcher. It didn't seem to work very well.

"Mum?"

"Yes?"

"What if when the bull comes into the ring, in a bullfight, and starts prancing around and tossing his head he's not angry at all? What if he's just playing? And what if he thinks the matador is playing as well? What if he thinks it's all a game?"

I thought she might be pleased I was finally asking something, but I guess these didn't really count as questions like all those "Why? Why? Why?" ones I never asked as a three-year old. For one thing, I didn't expect an answer.

And she didn't try to give me one. She thought for a moment, nodded slowly, and went off to toast the bagel.

Normally, when I'd meet up with Paige, I'd realize I hadn't missed her at all. But she was very cheery after the success of the last wish and spent most of the morning doodling with her gel pen. And at lunch she started talking with her mouth full, which is not something she normally does.

"The pens are super, aren't they?" she spluttered happily. "Oh, and even better news, my father may be coming home!"

"Wow. That's great. Is he feeling better?"

"I guess so. I wished for that, too, by the way. It was all by myself, but maybe Morgana heard me."

"And you think it's... safe?"

"Safe?"

"Him coming home, I mean, you know...with you mother still having all those mushrooms?"

"Oh, she wouldn't try that again." She was munching what looked like tuna mayonnaise, hopefully with no mushrooms in it. "We should be thinking about what we should wish for next."

"What if we've asked for so much she's going to be angry?" Maybe she should be. I could try that. I could just storm off and vanish.

"Why?"

"Because we've already had two."

"Three wishes," she insisted. "Everyone always gets three wishes."

"You said you wished for your father..."

"Well, that doesn't count! That was private. You weren't there!"

Ms. Patel handed out blue papers with some kind of table on them. And then she said we should compare something to something and make a list. And then the list would need to turn into lines on a graph. Or bars. Luckily, she didn't want us to start it now, we just had to copy down the numbers on the board, but I only got halfway through them when she erased it all, so in the end I just slipped the blue paper into my desk.

The next thing she was writing on the board was about the war called 1812.

But although sailors were getting kidnapped – which was interesting – I couldn't really listen properly while I was trying to come up with another favor a spirit might need and more importantly trying to think of a way to end the whole game without upsetting Paige too much.

We also got our spelling quiz back and I got 3/10 and Paige got 9/10. She looked at it open mouthed. Horrified. I wondered which one she got wrong but she quickly folded it in half and stuck it in a folder.

Just before the bell there was an announcement. A note had been found on the playground and Mr. Ruby, the principal, had it in his office so if the person who wrote it would like to have it back, they should come and collect it.

"I saw it," whispered Carl. "It said 'Mr. Ruby's a stupid Booby.'" Whispers and giggles flew round the class until the bell drowned them out.

"Was it you, Carl?" Phyllis gazed at him admiringly.

Carl looked scornful. "It's written in purple ink."

But Paige was pale as we walked out of the building. "I must have dropped it somewhere. The pen. Someone else must have found it."

It made me feel a little better to hear that I wasn't the only one who lost things and, although it shouldn't have, the note did, too.

May 7th: Maybe everyone gets called stupid sometimes.

CHAPTER FOURTEEN

We left our backpacks in my hall and went down the slope to the old split tree. I hauled myself up to the hollow seat nestled between the low branches and as I did my foot slipped and I scraped the whole side of one arm.

But the second I looked down to check if there was any blood, Paige was asking, "Is she there? Can she talk to us?"

So I dropped my head a bit more and closed my eyes. Then I hummed a little.

"Morgana?"

I opened my eyes to see Paige leaning on the trunk of the tree with her palms pressed against it almost like she was worshiping it. Or receiving an electrical charge. She was looking up hopefully. "Morgana?"

"I'm here."

"Thank you for coming."

"It is getting harder all the time."

"Why? Can we help? Can we do something for you?"

"No, no. Nothing."

"Nothing? There must be something!"

"Yes. Yes." I thought hard. "You can...pray for me." When my grandmother was over from Ireland, she taught me some prayers and took me to church. I liked it, but my mother wouldn't come with us.

"Pray? Why?"

"All spirits have to move on, you know, after a while, up to a higher level. And they need your prayers to help them."

"We don't want you to leave!"

"I'm sorry lass, I do have to."

"All right but if we do it, pray, I mean, can we have another wish?" she pleaded.

I really meant this to be the end and goodbye but Paige's eyes were blazing up at me. When she got upset they looked a bit crossed.

"Another wish?"

"Three wishes. You promised!"

I was pretty sure this wasn't true, but it was easier not to argue. "One last wish then. Just one." Then I let her fade out like the end of a song, "Pray for me, pray for..."

But Paige interrupted. "How do we pray? Where do we pray?"

"Rory will know," I managed and dropped my head again, slowly. When I brought my head back up, Paige was frowning.

"What did she say?" I asked.

"I thought you said you could hear her when you were in the trance."

"Yes, but not very clearly, I think she said..."

"That we have to pray for her. So, she can move up to another spirit level."

"Okay. I know how to do that."

"You do?" There was something like admiration in her eyes. That felt nice.

"We hafta set up a little shrine."

"A shrine?"

"Like an altar. We'll draw a picture of her..."

"We don't know what she looks like."

I almost thought I did, but I guess that was just me. "Well, we can just write her name on a piece of cardboard. And then put some wildflowers on either side and then we kneel down and say a prayer."

"Okay. And I'll write her name. My handwriting is better than yours."

I couldn't argue with that. "And I'll find a couple of jars for the flowers. Maybe you could bring a few from your greenhouse as well."

Paige awarded me a rare smile and tore off home.

When I got back to my house the twins were over. Stuart and Stephen were sitting in my living room doing their homework. I could hear our mothers' voices from the kitchen.

Stephen didn't look up, but Stuart did. "We're starting an Anti-Cruelty Society."

"To help animals?"

"People," said Stuart.

"Uh huh," agreed his brother.

"For instance, if we see one kid being crappy or shitty to another, we swoop in."

"Like bullies?" I didn't mean them. They looked confused.

"You mean being bullied. Yeah. Sort of like that. Or only if they're even screwing them over *mentally*. And you have to be a real detective to figure that out. You have to follow people. Then we'll have meetings and decide what to do."

"So, the fun part is spying."

"Yeah. By pretending you're not spying."

"Sounds tricky."

"Not really. You just ignore everybody. Pretend like they're not there. And then they don't pay attention to you, either."

Stephen finally looked up, "So, you want to join the club?"

"I'll think about it."

They went back to their homework. I stood there a minute more, but they didn't look back up or say anything else. They were good at ignoring people, all right.

As I passed the kitchen I could hear the twins' mother. "Girls are the best. You are so lucky. I was just desperate for a girl and look what I got."

"When Rory was born my first thought was ah, lovely, one day we'll be able to watch *Gone with the Wind* together. That's the whole point of having a girl, isn't it?"

"So have you watched it together, yet?"

"Yes, but she didn't like it at all!"

"No! I guess it's too late to change your mind and send her back?"

I was going to get a drink, but they were both laughing so hard I just went to my room.

May 9th: Tomorrow is another day. I think that was from that movie. They were all Irish, too.

CHAPTER FIFTEEN

We got our six-week report card that Friday. I meant to bring it home and was looking for it when Paige said to hurry up because the flowers she had brought for the shrine were wilting.

"I wish I was you," said Paige as we walked home. I was too surprised to answer her, but she went on. "Hey, that's it, maybe we should wish we could change places! I don't want to live in my house anymore. Could we do that?"

"Didn't you say your father is coming home?"

"I don't think he is. Not yet." She brightened up again. "I know, let's wish we can fly!"

Okay, that did it. I needed to make this the very, very last wish. "That's a great wish. But let's see how she feels today."

We'd made up our shrine to a made-up spirit in front of a bush down by the little creek at the bottom of the hill. And I'd made up a prayer based on a hymn my grandmother used to sing. We knelt down in front of it on a scatter of dry grass and I began:

> "May Morgana, like a dayspring,
> shine with Radiance Divine.
> and may she rise on high and bring
> the peace of Stars that Shine."

"What's a dayspring?" asked Paige.

"I think it's the feeling you get when the sun comes up on a new day." I remember when that was a good feeling, but that was a long time ago.

And then I felt the trance voice coming on without even thinking about it.

"Ah, that was lovely, lass," I said, as Morgana. "And that means Rory, *you* get the next wish." I wasn't in too much of a trance not to think of that.

Paige opened her mouth to speak, but Morgana looked right at her through dangerously slitted eyes, so she closed it again.

The next morning Paige was so early I hadn't finished eating my cereal. It still wasn't all that warm out, but I said that for my wish we really needed to be outside.

"What's the wish? Why won't you tell me?"

"Don't worry. It's a good one. I think you'll like it."

"I was thinking maybe I could wish my mother would get sick so I could go live with my father."

"I don't think that's the sort of wish we're allowed," I said as we wrapped scarves around our necks and went out to the sidewalk next to the twins' driveway.

"Well?" demanded Paige.

"Ready?"

"Ready."

"We wish to be invisible!!"

Paige gave a gasp of delight. "Oh yes! We wish to be invisible!" she cried.

"For a little while," I added quickly.

We stood breathing shallowly, not knowing where to look first. There was no one on the street. Then all at once we heard the thump of a basketball and Stuart and Stephen came charging out of their back door heading for the hoop above their garage. They shouted and laughed as they lurched through their first moves.

"Okay, here we go," I said, "Let's get closer."

We strolled up and stood a few feet from their game but neither boy so much as glanced our way.

And then it got even better. They stopped playing, and Stephen put his foot on the ball as they started arguing.

"This is a new game, Stu, you can't go and..."

"We were playing to ten."

"No, whoever gets five in a row..."

I waved. No response. And they were actually facing us now, flailing their arms around like mad. Then Stu knocked the ball out from under Stephen's foot and they went chasing it down the driveway.

Paige was beside herself. "We've done it! We're invisible!" She grabbed me in a hug and pulled me around in a circle. "Hey, can they hear our voices? Shout something. Go on. That will really freak them out."

"Hey guys, we wanna play!" I yelled.

Neither of them even looked around.

"This is great!" whooped Paige, then stopped. "But wait. I can see *you*."

This was a snag. "Right, but the important thing is, no one else can see us."

Then she looked around. "But there's no one else *not* to see us."

"But if we go up the street we'll find more people to not see us."

We walked quickly. There was a young man with a full-sized poodle who was pulling on the leash. He was muttering to the dog and didn't look up even though Paige broke into a run, giggling as she passed him.

"I bet he felt the wind as I rushed by and wondered what it was!"

"Yes, even his dog didn't see us and they notice everything!"

Paige was dancing with delight. "It's like we're ghosts."

Next, we passed a man washing his car. He didn't look up either. I was getting tenser by the minute.

Then she stopped dead and looked at me. "Let's do something really daring!"

"Like what?" Despite the chill I could feel sweat on the back of my neck.

"We could walk right into someone's house, sit down at their table and start eating..."

"Huh?"

"Or, wait, I know, we could go into a store and take anything we want!"

"Just a second, my sock is slipping down." I bent over and pretended to wiggle it back up over my heel.

"Hi Rory! Hi Paige!" called a voice from across the street. We both looked over to see little Abbey Benson and her mother getting into her car with a pile of library books. Her hair was really short now. Tanya called it a low-cost lawnmower special.

Paige looked at Abbey and then at me. Her face fell.

"I guess it's worn off," I said.

"Why?"

"We did say for "a little while.""

"No, you did. Why did you have to say that?"

"Did you want to be invisible for the rest of your life?"

She turned and started to head back to my house. When I caught up her voice had softened a bit. "Still, it really did work, didn't it? We really were invisible. For a little while."

"Of course we were."

"And it's my turn next time."

"What do you mean next time?"

"Well, the very first wish didn't count, and then there was that one my mother screwed up..."

"I don't think..."

"Don't try to think, Rory. Everyone knows it's hard for you."

She stomped off before I could answer. Not that there was an answer.

May 12th: Maybe one day I'll wake up and discover a part of my brain I never knew I had. And then everything will be different.

CHAPTER SIXTEEN

My mother once told Mr. C that I was very brave. She really meant braver than he thought I was. She told him about a time when I was seven or eight and we were walking with some of her grown up friends from the clinic, going down a grassy slope into the parking area. Somehow I tripped and went down and rolled over and over.

"Are you all right?" gasped Audrey, who was a nurse.

"I'm righter than right!" I'd said, managing to grin and bounce back up before hurrying on to the car ahead of them, trying hard not to limp.

The women murmured in admiration and my mother proudly said this showed that I had a fighting spirit.

All it really showed was that I was scared they would think I was clumsy. Or that they wouldn't like me. I don't think I have a fighting spirit. But I'm happy if Mr. C thinks I do. He likes to say things like "Much has been given to you and much will be expected of you." And "Remember you can't look weak. If you flinch, they smell blood, and they'll never leave you alone." Although for some reason almost everyone does leave me alone. Most of the time.

When I got home on Monday my mother was picking the mail up off the hall carpet. There was a letter with an Irish stamp. She kissed my hair and then sat down at the dining room table with it, but something about the way she was holding the paper made me stop and watch. Then her shoulders pinched in as if someone had opened a window and let in a sudden cold, black draft.

"Oh, Rory," her voice was tight and thin. "Mummy's dead." And she began to tremble. She squished the blue airmail paper into a tight ball like she was going to throw it away but instead held onto it even more fiercely.

She sat on the sofa and I stood close to her, helpless. I didn't want to ask how it had happened. I don't think Grandma was very old. And I had really liked her, although I'd only met her that once.

Mum swallowed at last and smiled a little and then she got up and went to the kitchen to make tea.

But later that night after I'd gone to bed, I heard her sobbing in her room. The door was closed, and it wasn't normal crying anymore. It was deep, gasping, heaving sounds.

I knocked a little on the door. But she called out for me to go away and leave her alone. She didn't say it like she knew who I was. Or wanted me for anything. Or even liked me.

The next day Mum seemed calmer again. She even smiled a little at breakfast. But it made my stomach tight to see the lines around her mouth where there normally aren't any.

I asked softly, "Why are you sad?"

She turned and stared at me, really hard. And this is exactly why I don't ask questions. Somehow, I use the wrong words. I don't say what I mean. I meant to say, "What are you remembering?" or "What are you thinking about that's hurting most?"

But she shook her head and repeated what I'd said with something like disgust. "Why am I *sad*? Because my mother died!"

Her eyes filled up again and she turned away. And then she burst out, "And I can't even go to the funeral because Aunt Nuula says they already had it. And she tells me this in a letter. Not a phone call. Or a text. Not even an e-mail. A letter! And she wasn't there, Rory. She wasn't even there; she wasn't even with her when she died!"

I was quiet for a while hoping to think of something that would help somehow and finally, I said, "I guess Grandma was the only person who really knew you when you were little."

"What?" She was looking at me again, but gentler now, more like she was surprised.

"I mean," I took a breath and tried to get the words right. "She knew you when you were a baby and she was the only one who knew everything you did. And when you did it. What you laughed at. And what made you happy."

"Yes." She was looking like I'd said something unusual even though it was a completely normal thought once I got it out. "You're right. Oh, Rory, and I never asked her nearly enough about my childhood, and now it's too late. That's all gone. When your mother dies, all her memories die, too."

"I never met Aunt Nuula."

"She wanted to call you Bridget," Mum smiled a bit at last. "But we were already over here and there wasn't a damn thing she could do."

"Bridget?"

"I wanted Ciara, but your Dad thought it might be a worry to you. Hard for people to spell."

Just as well, then. "It's okay. I like Aurora."

"Aurora?"

"My full name. Aurora."

Her eyes started to fill up again. "Oh no, honey. It's just Rory."

"But Daddy told me..."

"Your Daddy was a great leg puller altogether."

So. Not Aurora then. Nobody's Dawn after all.

I slipped out after dinner to visit Mrs. Harvey's hive. It was dark and there wasn't any sign that there were any bees living there at all. But she had told me they sleep, like we do, for hours at a time. Sometimes in the daytime, even, out working, taking a break, curling up in a flower.

I didn't have a black ribbon but I brought a black sock, an odd one that I found in my drawer and I laid it on the ground under the box and said quietly, "My grandmother died. She was here once. She came for a visit, and you may have seen her. I just thought I'd let you know."

That night Mr. C came and stayed over, which he doesn't often do during the week. And I didn't mean to listen but I did for a while. They didn't seem to be really talking, but they must have been because every now and then one of them would kind of murmur or sigh or something. I was just happy that for once it was nothing to do with me.

The next morning Mum felt well enough to go through my backpack before I left for school. She knew the report card was supposed to be in there because I had brought a note home about it the week before. I wasn't hiding it. I just wasn't sure where it was.

She never did find it so at lunchtime she came over to the school. There were lots of people around, in the classroom and in the corridor where my locker is. Most people don't really lock them, they're just called that.

There was a thin drizzle of rain starting and I was just about to get my jacket out and go into the playground when I saw her coming down the corridor. For an instant I was as happy as someone who's spotted a ship coming to pick them up off a desert island. I stood smiling as she came up.

"So, is this your locker?" She reached for the handle. She opened it.

There's a shelf above where the coat hooks are and it was piled with papers and envelopes. And the lower part where you put your boots and shoes was crammed with books and folders.

She stared at me and then she began yanking it all out. The whole mess. Everything came crashing to the floor. She seized an envelope and waved it in my face.

"What's this?"

I didn't answer. She told me anyway. "It's the order for the chocolates!" She ripped it open, "And the money's still in here! There's twenty-five dollars here! Cash. You never handed it in!"

"I'm sorry."

"That was three weeks ago. The fundraiser is over. What were you thinking?!" She was breathing hard and kneeling there in the corridor with some kids staring at us and some trying not to stare at us. "And here are all the instructions Doug gave you on the games for the Fair! You were supposed to..."

And so it went on. There was homework there I'd never done and even some homework I had done but never handed in. And of course there was the envelope with the report card.

She finally stood up and said in a voice I'd never heard before but at least it wasn't loud, "I want you to go through all of this and put it in order and have it done by the time I get back." She took the money and the report card and went to find Ms. Patel and left me standing there.

I didn't know what to do with all the old papers, so I sat there just slowly smoothing them out and making a lumpy pile when suddenly Paige was kneeling beside me. She didn't say anything, but she helped me sort the papers - the things that belonged in the classroom and the things that should have gone home and the things that were so old it didn't matter where they should have gone. There were some library books as well and she took those back for me.

My mother and Doug were hugging each other when I got home. I left the door open so they wouldn't hear it close and stayed in the hall where they couldn't see me.

He said:	Don't be so hard on yourself. You have to scare them sometimes. You're her parent, not her friend.
She said:	But it's just the two of us. We only have each other.
He said:	You have me.

She said:	I never told you. I had a little baby brother. He died when I was six. In Ireland. The thing is, everyone said he wasn't quite "right."
He said:	Not right?
She said:	He didn't smile. He never wanted to be held. When I picked him up he would arch his back and pull away and go stiff as a board.

I was sure she was going to say, "Of course Rory's nothing like that." Because I'm not. But she didn't. They were just quiet. And they stayed quiet. Neither of them spoke to me all evening and the next morning I couldn't get out of bed. My throat was burning, and my head was hurting as if I had thoughts I couldn't think and words I couldn't say. Mum said it might be strep and she would phone me in sick.

It was already Thursday and Mr. C, who had stayed over again, said I might as well take the rest of the week off since my class was taking standardized tests for two days and it would be better for me not to do them since I'd only bring the rating of the whole school down. That night I huddled into the bedclothes until I was as small as I could make myself and kept the coverlet over my head.

May 17th: I wish I was a squirrel and could stay curled up in a warm nest and never have to go to school.

CHAPTER SEVENTEEN

My mother once said I was enough to make a cat laugh. I know she meant this as a nice thing to say because we were joking around. Since she looked so pleased it seemed a good time to ask her if I could have a kitten. I said it would be fun to see a real one laugh. But she just looked sad and said animals tie you down. I haven't asked again.

But a cat would never think you were second best and never ask, "Why did you do that?" or "What were you thinking?"

Since my mother began talking to me again she's started asking if I want to take art, or singing, or even horse riding after school or on Saturday. "You're good at art, you sing well. You like animals."

I used to go to dance classes. When I was five or six. I liked those. But it was Daddy who used to drive me and after that I didn't go anymore.

"I'm not sure."

"People do try new things, Rory, even when they're not sure." She said she just wanted me to work on things I'm good at to boost my confidence. She said it wouldn't take much. "You used to have so much confidence when you were little," she said.

That didn't make me feel any better.

"Now we have the shrine to Morgana, we should pray to her as well as for her." Paige chirped. "And I can pray that my father comes home because that's not a wish. And the great thing is she's really here, with us, not like Jesus or God."

My heart seems to beat faster than it should a lot of the time but especially when I was with Paige. "Slow down, I feel funny."

"What kind of funny?" Her concern was impatient.

"Dizzy," I said. "I feel very lightheaded." A solution had begun to form in my mind.

"Will you come on? We're almost there!"

"Paige!" I said in a low growly voice. "Stop walking. We haven't been introduced."

She turned and stared. "What's the matter with you?"

"Morgana cannot be contacted today. It is forbidden."

"Who are you?" she asked in awe.

"You can call me... Cameo."

"What do you want from us?"

"Do you want to help Morgana?"

"Of course. Is she in trouble? Is it because of us?"

"Follow me."

We went down into the woods. "Stand there," I told her, pointing to a bush with plump white berries on it, the kind you pop with your fingers. Then I went over to an old truck tire which used to be a swing and was now angled up against a log. I kicked it three times making three satisfying thumps, then I put one foot up on it like a heroic statue.

"Silence! You are now in the presence of the Spirit Court. You will be asked to testify in a few moments."

Paige flushed and was still.

I used to watch a TV show that had trials in it, and I could hear the words clearly in my head. "We understand, your Honors, that our client Morgana is being held on suspicion of becoming too involved with mortals and that she has broken your code by granting several of their childish requests, which I believe they call 'wishes.' In Morgana's defense I would like to call Miss Paige Worthing. Please stand Miss Worthing."

Paige squinted around, shivering. "I am standing," she whispered. "Where are they?"

"Can't you see them?"

She shook her head. "Over there," I said, pointing to a cleft between two small evergreens. Their shadowy branches swayed. There was a pause. Then I frowned at her. "You are being addressed, Miss Worthing. You must reply."

"Oh! What did they ask? I'm sorry."

"You can't hear them?"

Paige shook her head miserably.

"You are being asked if you are willing to testify under oath?"

"Do I answer you, or the Court?"

"They can hear you," Cameo replied. I was trying to keep things as uncomplicated as possible.

"Then yes, I am."

"Do you, by all that you believe in, swear to tell the truth, the whole truth and nothing but the truth?"

Paige raised her right hand timidly. "I do."

"If it please the Court," I added, "I will conduct the cross-examination myself." I realized afterward I should probably have just said "examination" (without the "cross" part) but Paige didn't seem to notice. "How long have you been acquainted with the defendant, Morgana?"

"About two months. I think."

"Would you tell the Court of your dealings with her in that time?"

"The first thing I remember was the picture. We wished for a picture like the one which Rory drew in class." She looked around, worried. "Where is Rory?"

"She is here."

"Can she hear this?"

"Yes. Go on."

Paige swallowed. "Well, it wasn't Rory who wished for it. It was me. I wanted to find out if Morgana could really grant wishes. And I thought she might be more likely to if it was to get us out of a tight spot."

"Why were you in a tight spot?"

"I had promised the picture to the teacher, at school."

"So you admit it was you who put Morgana in this "tight spot" as you call it."

"Yes."

I turned to her and held up my hand and said the judges were discussing this point, but it sounded like they agreed the incident was not entirely the defendant's fault.

"What do they look like?" whispered Paige.

"Spirits. Now, what happened next?"

"We got... I got a note from Morgana."

"Saying what?"

"That she didn't see why she should help us, since she was only allowed to help friends and relatives."

I held up my hand again as if the judges were surprised and muttering about this. Then I smiled and nodded to them and told her to go on.

"So," she hesitated, "we ended up delivering a message for her."

"Why couldn't she deliver it herself? Why did she need you?"

Paige thought about this earnestly. "I think she did it to test our loyalty. To see if she could trust us."

I looked at the Spirit Court and pretended they were in an uproar at this. Paige was biting her lip. "It's all right. They are speaking directly to Morgana now. Yes. She has confirmed what you say and thanks you for your belief and support."

Paige nodded in relief. "And after that she granted us three wishes."

"Just three? What were they?"

"My china horses came to life, we got two amazing new pens, and we became invisible."

I beamed at her approvingly. "Thank you, Miss Worthing. You were the star witness. Now we just have to wait."

We did. Paige really could be very patient when she tried.

"They are prepared to deliver the verdict now." I listened respectfully. "I see. Yes. Morgana has been a little too generous with you, so we have decided on an early promotion to the next spirit level, the Summerlands, where contact with the Earth will be very difficult."

Paige gave a little cry.

"The court will now rise."

Paige had been standing the whole trial anyway so she just bowed her head as I took my foot off the tire.

"Wow!" I said in my own voice.

"Rory?" I nodded. "Oh, Rory!" And she threw her arms around me and hugged me.

And then I thought I saw a flash of something red behind the hollow tree, but I wasn't sure then. Now I am.

I thought I'd sent Morgana to a distant, far, far away place where she couldn't grant anyone any more wishes. But then Paige got a letter. From Cameo.

We were about to go through the glass doors into the school when she jumped in front of me from nowhere waving a piece of paper. She found it in her backpack and now she was rushing right past 'excited' and headed straight for 'hyper' while I was trying hard to read it.

It wasn't in the wavy writing I had used for Morgana. It was pencil and very faint and it was in a nice round style like on the label of Mrs. Harvey's honey.

And I didn't write it.

Dear Paige,
Since you were so honest at the trial, we will grant one more wish after all. But first we require a sacrifice.
Think carefully,
Cameo.

"Isn't this great? And I know what to wish for!"

"Hold on. Forget the wish for a minute. A sacrifice?" Had the twins been spying on us? Who else could have written it? I looked at her in alarm. "Paige, we're supposed to make a sacrifice."

"Well, we can do that." She picked up her backpack and pushed the door open.

May 21st: If I could live in a story, it wouldn't be this one.

CHAPTER EIGHTEEN

My mother has never been any good at hiding her feelings and since the thing with my locker (and Grandma) it's as if she wants to spread the hurt around. Or the blame.

Like when we were driving to the store in Doug's car and she suddenly said, "Oh look, there's a little white cat sitting right on top of that bird feeder, do you see? Stop, Doug, can you? I want to take a picture!"

But he just made a face and said, "It's rush hour, Katie."

She sat looking back over her shoulder. "But it was a perfect shot. And I'll never get a chance at it again. I wanted it for the calendar. Damn it, Doug, I don't ask for much!"

"Sorry, I can't turn around now."

"I should have been driving. Then I could stop whenever I wanted to!"

And then she was very quiet until she went into the dry-cleaning store and came out with my winter coat and something else, something in her hand. She held it up. It was the audio recorder.

"You said you lent it to someone," said Doug, not sounding very surprised.

"She gave it back." I managed. "Sorry, I didn't mean to leave it in..."

"How long have you had it back? The last time you wore this coat was months ago. Why didn't you check the pockets? Why didn't I check the pockets?" She slammed the car door.

There was more to come when we got home.

He said:	You should get her tested. I mean it.
She said:	I've had her tested. Last year. They weren't sure. They said she maybe has a bit of... something.
He said:	She has more than a bit of something!
She said:	Sure they said they think she may be... that thing.
He said:	On the spectrum.
She said:	But I don't want her labeled. Why does everyone have to be labeled?
He said:	So she can be helped.

But then Ms. Patel asked my mother to come for an interview. It wasn't the normal one at the end of a term, so I wasn't sure if I should come or not. In my school it's okay if the kids are there, although it's up to the parents. My mother said of course she wanted me to come.

Ms. Patel started out by looking straight at me and saying kindly that I was "unique." I didn't say anything, but my mother nodded, so Ms. Patel turned to her. "But you have been made aware there is some sort of neurodivergence."

"Yes," agreed my mother evenly.

"And ever since her special educational plan was set up, she's been given extra time."

"I know," said my mother. Now it was like I wasn't there after all.

"But even with one-on-one help we can't pretend she is thriving. She often doesn't get beyond the first page on tests."

This is true. Not because I don't know some of the answers but because there are too many words and sentences to sort out all at once. Multiple choice is the worst.

"The thing I want to talk to you about," said Ms. Patel, glancing at me as if she had no idea where I'd suddenly appeared from, "is, well…"

"Yes?" asked my mother.

"It's beginning to look like Rory is not going to be able pass this school year."

"Pardon?'

"She won't be able to move up. Not here."

I stared at the equations on the blackboard.

"She's supposed to be permitted to stay here in school with her friends…"

"We have tried, but I thought from the reports you've been getting, and the notes we've been sending home, you'd have some idea. We believe that Rory needs not only a special program, but a special school."

I stared at the fish tank. I'd never have a real graduation. Not now, and not from High School later. No special dress. No robe. I wouldn't walk up the steps onto the stage with the others with music playing. Or go to a dance in the gym after.

I swallowed. "Mum. Couldn't I... Maybe, maybe if I... tried harder."

But Ms. Patel just looked at me with pity, like you would at a monkey who was asking to fly a jet.

"The trouble is," said my mother, standing up. "You don't consider imagination and intuition a form of genius."

Then she did that thing with her eyes that meant *Let's go, we're done here* and thanked Ms. Patel in a soft voice, and I followed her out.

May 25th: If I had a brother or sister then at least my mother would have one smart child.

CHAPTER NINETEEN

I didn't know which was worse: failing school or wondering what kind of sacrifice Paige might come up with. The kind where you give something up? Or the kind where you do something to some poor little creature? Does belief really need something horrible to happen to make it work? Does a miracle?

"So! Roaring Rory!" I heard Stuart and Stephen calling from their back porch. As I got closer, I could see they were practicing throwing a pocketknife into a stump but I had to get even closer so I could talk without shouting. As usual they went first.

"Your friend is a real disaster," sneered Stuart.

"That's my problem."

"You can get rid of her if you join our club."

"You wrote that note."

"What note?" They looked at each other and started snorting in such an explosive way that snot shot out of Stephen's nose.

"We're here for you!" Stuart called after me as I stumbled away. The ground was so rough I cut back to their driveway, then stopped because I almost trod on a little dead bird.

I knew it was a chickadee because Mr. C always pointed out their striped caps whenever he saw them. They sometimes sing in the evergreen branches outside my window.

Anyway, it hadn't been run over because it wasn't squashed, and I was just picking it up to put it in the bushes when I saw its leg tremble a little. I cradled it against me for a few moments and felt a faint flutter of its wings. It was like life was flowing right back into it from the warmth of my chest. And then, suddenly, it started struggling so hard I thought it would hurt itself.

The sun was strong, so I put it down at the base of a tree and sure enough it tottered up onto its feet and looked at me for a long time. Well, I'm not sure how long. It felt like a long time. Then, all at once, it opened its wings and took off.

I felt a bit better then, almost strong enough to go back and try to tell them to stop spying on us. Mr. C. said I should never flinch. Then again, they might have had enough fun by now and they'd just quit by themselves. They did get bored easily.

When I got back to the house my mother was just finishing up on the phone, saying, "Of course I understand. Of course I will. Thanks again, and I'm so sorry to hear it. Take care. All the best, the best of luck now."

She hung up and looked at me as I took off my boots.

"That was Paige's mother," she began. "She was just letting me know. Did you know?"

"Know what?"

"That they're getting divorced. Paige's mother and father."

"But he's in hospital!"

"He's not in hospital." She frowned. "He's in Vancouver. They've been separated for months. She and Paige moved here when they split up. Now he wants a divorce. It's very sad. And Mrs. Worthing was just letting me know in case, well, in case Paige seems upset, or acts strangely. "

Paige was always acting strangely.

"So, we must be very kind to her, I think," she said, turning to butter a piece of toast. "Not that you aren't. You're always kind."

"She doesn't like her mother."

"Of course she does. She's a lovely woman. Though I think they were closer. Paige and her father, I mean."

I looked at the floor and she came over and touched my shoulder. "I know how much things can hurt, but in the end there's not so much so very serious that can happen to you at your age. You're still so lucky."

I didn't feel lucky.

"You lied about your mother."

"What?"

"She's good to you."

"That's not true."

"And you're father's not in hospital."

Paige flinched. "How do you know?"

"Everyone knows." I lowered my voice. "We've always known."

"We? Oh wait, you're not Rory. You're Cameo!" She was trembling now. I thought if Cameo came on strong enough, and was angry enough, we wouldn't have to do the sacrifice at all, or make another wish. "Rory, please come back!"

I took a step away, slowly, shaking my head as if to clear it and get rid of the invading spirit. She looked relieved but her eyes were rimmed with red.

"Why did you lie about your father?" I asked. But then I thought maybe she didn't know.

"I didn't. She did poison him, that's why he went away!"

"I don't believe you."

"No, you never do!"

Now I think about it we were probably making so much noise there was no way we would have known if anyone was watching us. But they were.

"I don't care! I want to make the sacrifice now!"

"What kind of sacrifice?" I was trying not to picture a crow, bloody feathers flying. "I don't want to hurt anything!"

"Not a blood sacrifice, stupid. An offering. Come on."

What the spirits wanted was definitely getting mixed up with what Paige wanted. "Where?"

But she went trudging on down to the small muddy creek at the bottom of the hill. It wasn't much, just a trickle jammed between the rows of houses and there was already somebody's offering of shopping cart in it. And there were little puddles of standing water because it had just rained.

"You always make offerings in water," she said. "We have to be very still. I will say the words."

I swallowed and stood facing the creek in as respectful a stance as I could manage with one boot inching slowly down the bank.

"We have come to make a solemn offering to the Spirits." Her voice was high and tense. "We ask that we be allowed to make this offering and that it will be acceptable to you."

We waited.

Suddenly we heard something like a twig cracking a little way off which Paige seized upon as a sign. "You are listening! Thank you! You are here. We shall make the sacrifice now!"

Her hand went to her neck, and she unzipped her jacket just enough so that her gold necklace slipped out. She nodded to me. I stared at it.

"Take it," she commanded. "Go on. Pull it off!" I took a step backward. But she grabbed my hand and pulled it to her throat, hissing. "I mean it, do it, or I'll never speak to you again."

I took the chain and pulled a bit.

"Harder!" She said through clenched teeth, and I gave a sharper tug and a link of the chain must have broken because suddenly it was in my hand, sapphire and all. But it wasn't in my hand long. She seized it and flung it in a glinting arch, and we watched it come down into a watery pool of mud. Where it sank.

Then she crumbled and began to cry.

"What did you do that for? I thought your father gave that to you!"

"I had to. It's the most precious thing I have," she sobbed. "And now I'm going to make a wish."

"We have to talk about it first..."

"No! I made the sacrifice. This is my wish. Not yours." She took a deep breath. "I want to go and live with my father."

"Okay, well," I was flooded with relief. "I'll help. We wish..."

"Stop it! That's not the wish."

"What is?"

"I want my mother to get sick."

"What? Why?"

"Then I'll be allowed to go, get it? Maybe she should even die."

"No!"

"I wish my mother would get sick and die!" she cried out to the rustling branches above us.

"No, no...we don't wish that..."

"Yes, we do! I do!"

I stood open mouthed as she zipped her jacket and turned to me completely calmly and smiled. "How long do you think it will take to work?"

My mother says that when you are afraid you can't hear your heart speak. You have to keep very still to let that small inner voice tell you what you need. She said it can even tell you what to do.

May 26th: I haven't heard my heart say anything in a really long time.

CHAPTER TWENTY

Paige was absent again on Monday and when I got to her house her mother answered the door.

"I'm afraid we're in a bit of a mess here at the moment," she said as she let me in.

She must have still been feeling pretty healthy because she was in the middle of painting. There was a large can of turquoise paint and a sheet of plastic and a roller pan in the doorway to the kitchen. She stepped around it all neatly, no problem with her balance or anything. "Paige is in her room. I'll bring you up some hot chocolate."

"Thanks, but I don't think I can stay long," I called as I scooted up the stairs. The door was closed. I knocked and a faint voice told me to come in.

Paige was sitting on her bed with a piece of paper in her hand. It was the same kind of paper the first note had been on. And the same pencil writing with the round letters.

"I found this note. In my pocket. It says I'm evil. Selfish and cruel and evil and I must be punished." She looked up at me. "Help me, Rory," she whispered. "I need you. Please? Please?" It was a tiny, terrible sound. She looked thinner. She was shivering in a light shirt and I could see scratch marks on her arms.

"What can I do?"

"They hate me. The spirits. They say I'm worthless." She thrust the paper at me.

One of the scratches popped a few beads of fresh blood as she stretched out her arm.

"Spoilt, arrogant, willful," I read. You could tell the twins went to private school. They went on to say that the failure of the wishes was due to her 'disgraceful personality' and that all future contact with the spirit world was forbidden by 'higher powers than the writer was at liberty to name'.

"You didn't get one, too... did you?" she asked, suddenly hopeful.

"No." Then I thought maybe I should have said I did, she was so miserable. And I was too.

"It's not like we wished for riches beyond our wildest dreams or a castle in Scotland. We didn't even wish that we could fly!"

"I know, let's find the chain! Then we can take the last wish back."

"We can't. It was two days ago. And it's been raining."

"Tomorrow. After school. We have to try."

She flopped back on the bed. The shadows and angles of her face made her look even thinner. We should have had the hot chocolate.

That night I took one of the steak knives from the kitchen drawer and snuck it into my room. I was numb with the small, dull hope that it would help. Maybe I'd feel something. Relief. Or calm.

I sat up with my back against the pillows and made the first little cut, waiting for the pain and wondering if it would be a warm thing. Or cold. But as I watched the blood seep up like a row of tiny seeds, my mother knocked on the door.

I shoved the knife under the edge of the duvet and turned my arm over and pressed my other hand over the cut.

"Can I come in?" she said. "I just made a cup of tea."

"Okay." She put the mug down on my headboard, and asked if she could sit on my bed for a moment. I tugged the duvet toward me, but she'd already sat on it which pulled it so tight I could see the tip of the handle of the knife.

She was saying I mustn't forget that poets believed the whole world is balanced on a fairy's wing although only children seemed to remember it these days. Which made me forget the knife and for some reason remember a morning when my father sat reflecting a sunbeam off the glass face of his watch, laughing as he teased me that it was a real fairy dancing across the living room wall. I had believed him. I always believed him.

She sighed and added that most grown-ups act like they want to crush all the excitement out of being alive. Her eyes were very sad as she said this. She didn't seem very excited to be alive right then either. And then she added, really quietly, "And what's that knife doing here?"

"I don't know."

"And why are you holding your arm?"

"I..."

"There's blood under your hand." She leapt up, flinging the duvet back and picking up the knife. "What gave you this idea? Or should I say *who*?"

"No one."

"Well, someone surely did because you didn't go and think something like that up by yourself, did you? No one says to themselves, 'You know what? I fancy dragging a blade over my skin here and there to draw up a wee bit of blood.' Of course, you heard about it somewhere and you thought 'Right, now that's a brilliant little trick I have to try.' Well?"

I didn't say anything.

She took another breath. "How would you feel if you saw me slicing up my own arm? Or if you walked in on your teacher doing it? And couldn't you think of something more original? Do you have to be doing something because someone else is doing it? Are you nothing more than a sad, wee, mindless copycat? No, not my child. You are better than this!"

And she stormed out. Without the knife.

Two minutes later she was back, her face like chalk and her voice low and shaky. She hugged me and said she was sorry but seeing me want to hurt myself was like watching someone spray-painting four letter words on the Taj Mahal. Or taking a hammer to the statue of David in Florence. It was a sacrilege, and she couldn't bear it.

She said of course I hurt. She knew I hurt. But if I hurt that badly we needed to do something. And we would think of something. She just didn't know what. She just didn't know.

I didn't know either.

May 27th: Now we're both afraid and it's all my fault.

CHAPTER TWENTY-ONE

On Monday Paige did make it to school after all, and I did too, although I spent most of the time in the girls' washroom. I skipped three classes in a row and no one seemed to notice. I just lay down on the polished cement floor which was cool under my cheek. Tanya came in but she was alone, so she pretended she didn't see me.

I did come out for lunch, but I didn't want anything. Paige sat next to me but never said a word. And she only managed to eat half of a half of a sandwich.

After school we found some old boots and went down and tried to stand exactly where we stood on Saturday, but of course the rain had moved everything around on the bank. We took sticks and gently stirred around in the place we thought the necklace had vanished and dredged up a broken piece of bottle and a rusty Sprite can. We finally got to our knees and yanked off our gloves and were panting and pulling up handfuls of sludge when we heard their voices.

"Hand her over!" thundered Stuart.

"Citizen's arrest!" yelled Stephen.

"What do you want?" I started backing away.

"Give us the brat!"

"Yes, get out of our way or you'll be an accomplice!"

"And a traitor!!"

"Traitor?"

"To the Society for the Prevention of Cruelty."

"Yeah, Rory, you should be grateful. We heard the way she's treated you. We heard every word!" They shoved me away so hard my boots slid away on the soft ground, and I went down hard on my back.

Then they yelled, "Stay out of it, Rory! It's her we want." The edge of the stream still had a brittle crusty ridge of mud and Stephen was grinding some up into a ball.

Hands on hips, Stuart watched, grinning.

"If we still had snow we could fasten her to the back of a sled and drag her round the park, like Hector round the walls of Troy!"

Then Paige was clutching my arm. Helping me up.

"Let go of her, you bossy, creepy little coward! Don't pretend to be some kind of totally amazing friend to her now!"

Paige was trembling. She let go of me and they began to prance menacingly around her. As I got to my knees, they grabbed her by the scruff of her jacket, and started forcing large handfuls of mud down the back of her neck.

"Hey, let's mud-wash her mud-mouth out with slime!" They yanked her head back to cram the cold dirt against her teeth and lips. She sputtered, but only faintly, as if even the smallest protest was against her will. Then she just sagged and crumpled down out of their arms. And when Stuart put a foot on her back and forced her down further, she didn't resist.

I crawled toward her, "Paige? Paige!" But if she was even conscious, she gave no sign and all the while her tormentors kept on shoveling wet earth on her like a team of gravediggers. Her blonde hair was matted and gray.

"Stop it, stop it...you'll suffocate her!" I was up now, flailing at them wildly.

They straightened resentfully and stood back a bit, genuinely surprised.

"Oh, she's all right, she's not hurt," grumbled Stephen.

"But has she learned her lesson? That's the question." Stuart nudged her with his boot. There was no response. Paige was motionless, the few visible bits of her face blotched and pink.

Stephen stepped back, out of the ring of trampled mud. "Oh, come on, Stu," he said gruffly. "Let's go and shoot some hoops."

"This was supposed to be fun. Girls. Geez." They turned on their heels and trudged back up the bank.

Paige only stirred when their voices died away. I bent down to help her as she struggled to her feet. She let me do that.

"I'll take you home. Paige? I'll tell. I'll go tell. Who should I tell?"

She pushed me away, gently. "No one. You can't tell... Ever."

"Why?"

"She wouldn't like it."

"Who?" But she went wandering and slipping slowly up the hill without speaking again, or glancing back.

And then all I could hear was a noise like a high-pitched whine. It took a while to realized it was coming from me, from my throat. I fell to my knees and rocked back and forth. I thumped my head and cheeks with my fists, but nothing helped.

I was scared to go back to the house because there was nothing my mother could do. There was nothing anyone could do. It would be better to lie down under a tree. Maybe misery could help you die. I didn't want to be there. I didn't want to be anywhere.

I stumbled over to the fence and pushed through to the hive, coming what I hoped was much too close, and lay down in front of it.

Mrs. Harvey said that bees hate loud noises so if you're going to use a lawnmower you should always wait until all the bees come back at night and then lock them up until the next day otherwise they can get angry and swarm out and sting you.

I wanted them to sting me. So, I made even more noise, sobbing as loudly as I could. Sure enough, where at first there were just a few bees hovering around the entrance suddenly there were dozens, and more coming tumbling out after them.

But instead of flying at me in a rage they all turned their backs and perched there. And then they began to fan their wings, vibrating them until they built up a whole, perfect wall of sound. And slowly, very slowly I began to hear them more than I could my own wailing and I started to quiet down, drifting with their deep, pulsing hum.

Even after I stopped shivering, I stayed there, close, muddy and cold, but listening until at last the hive grew quiet and the sun was almost down.

And then I went home. My mother stared at my clothes and ran me a hot bath. She didn't say anything but her eyebrows were higher than normal and twitching from time to time.

When I went to bed, I prayed hard that when I woke up they would tell me that there was no Paige and never had been, and that I had made the whole thing up.

But the trouble with trouble is, it's real. It's never something you make up. Especially when you're the one who makes it.

May 28th: I have an idea. But it probably won't work.

CHAPTER TWENTY-TWO

Mum said I didn't have to go to school for the rest of the week which was good but it was only two days. She said she wanted to stay with me and kept asking what had happened, that I was all scraped and muddy and that she was sorry but she still had to go to work.

I didn't tell her about the twins. I said Paige and I fell out of the old split tree. The first day I spent by myself at home, which was awful, but better than school.

When I looked at my hands, my fingers were shaking, and I couldn't stop them and I took a couple of Tylenol mashed up in peanut butter because I can never swallow pills. But that was all I ate all day.

The second day my fingers were steadier, and the rain had stopped and I hurried back down to the creek. I stood and stared at the whole muddy mess where the twins had ganged up on Paige. But there were other, clearer tracks now the sun was out and the ground was getting dry.

I was pretty sure I could tell the place where Paige and I stood when she threw her necklace, though there were also a lot of deep footprints from when we came back and had been crouching down, digging around in the pools trying to find it again.

But I had it in my head that this time I could find it. It was just this feeling. A feeling that I would find it. If I did it in a different way.

There was a huge arched tree root sticking up out of the ground, which I used to straddle like a horse when I was little. Now I sat on it with my back very straight and my hands on my knees. And I stared out over the creek.

"I wish to find Paige's necklace," I whispered. "I wish to find it and have it right here in my..."

"What are you doing?" asked a light voice behind me.

I turned, startled. But it was only little Abbey Benson, looking even smaller than usual now it was warm enough she didn't have her big parka on, and her long hair was gone. Or maybe she was an elf or a fairy, come to trick me, and not Abbey at all. But she smiled to show me she was definitely just Abbey. "What are you doing?"

"Nothing."

"Can I help?"

"Not really."

She plonked herself down beside me anyway and pointed up at something.

"You see that black squirrel?"

"Yes." It was just above us, up on its hind legs, begging, frozen, watching.

"I wish we could be friends with wild animals, don't you?" I looked up at the squirrel and tried to picture it coming closer. You could almost say I was *wishing* it would. And we both held our breath and sure enough, it dropped slowly onto its forepaws and started down the bark, head first, step by step until it was only two or three feet from Abbey. Of course, then she squeaked really loudly so the squirrel turned tail and bolted, but her eyes were glowing anyway.

"You can do things, can't you? Strange things. Everyone says."

"Why? They don't know anything about me."

She squinted up at the leaves which were pretty much fully out by now and a ray of sun glinted on the lens of her glasses. "Do you think trees worry about which one of them is the tallest?" I shook my head.

She sighed. "I do, though."

"Sure, but... you'll be a different height tomorrow. Even if it's only a kitten's whisker every day, you just wait and watch how it all adds up."

She nodded, which made me feel better since it seemed to make her feel better, but of course, by now, I was completely distracted from why I was there. "Now, if you want to help, can you be really still? Just for a little while?"

She nodded. "I'll close my eyes." And I went back to staring at the bank and wishing for the necklace, over and over, but this time silently, in my head.

A few minutes passed and Abbey was good and quiet. But then her eyes popped open again.

"I have to go."

"Okay."

"No, I mean I have to go pee."

"Here?"

"No, I'll go home. Maybe I'll see you here again? And we could play something else?" She got up and took a step backward, waving her arm in the direction of the tiny stream. "We could build little toy boats, maybe, and race them — " But then I leaped up because when she flung her arm out, she slipped and sat down hard in the stony mud.

"Ow!" She looked down at the hand that broke her fall. "Oh no, I think I cut myself on something, look it's sharp and..." And she slowly raised the hand and there, dangling from it was the gold necklace with the blue sapphire, winking in the sun.

Half an hour later I was pushing the doorbell at Paige's. I hadn't called first. My heart was cramping and sore with how much I wanted to try to make things better. To explain that the trouble we were in was mostly my fault. Or all my fault. I would start by telling her that my name wasn't Aurora. That it was just Rory. Plain Rory.

I was almost leaning on the door when Mrs. Worthing opened it, looking just as calm as always. She always talked like she was measuring out her words, one at a time. I wondered what it would be like to have a mother like that.

"Paige isn't here, dear." she smiled.

"Oh."

"She left this morning for Vancouver. I'm sorry. I should have phoned your mother. We decided at the very last minute, and I forgot you were coming. We had so much to do with all the packing. She's gone to stay with her dad for the summer."

I was standing in the hall, but I could see right through into the kitchen. And there was something very wrong in there.

"Would you like a cup of cocoa? Keep your shoes on, dear, I'm not sure I've picked all the glass up yet." I couldn't believe she asked me in.

The whole kitchen, floor to ceiling - the stove, the refrigerator and countertops – everywhere – was splashed with zigzags of turquoise paint. The windows had been gobbed over with big brushfuls of it and the drips had run until they'd dried like big blue scabs. The door was splotched with handprints. Paige's handprints.

Mrs. Worthing put the kettle on.

"I think I swept up most of the plaster but of course you just never know with glass. She didn't get it on her clothes though, which was a mercy."

"Who?"

"Why Paige, of course. But then she's always been good with her clothes. Very careful." She took out a tub of hot chocolate powder and found a spoon while I stared from her to the open can of paint lying empty on its side on a pile of newspaper. She was almost smiling, as if Paige hadn't done anything more unusual than knocking over a bowl of cereal.

"I think I'll get some professionals in to finish up now," she said. "I wasn't looking forward to doing it myself anyway, so this is really a blessing in disguise."

Mrs. Worthing poured the water slowly. "And you know, now I see it, I'm not that sure about the color anymore anyway."

"Is Paige all right?"

"I think she might have been a bit upset about something that had happened at school. She didn't say what. And I don't suppose you'd tell me; I know how you kids are. Can't get a word out of you. It's a shame she won't finish the year, but she gets such good grades, school really isn't a challenge for her."

"Did she say anything about me?"

"Did she? Yes, that's right. She said to be sure to tell you, oh, what was it now? I know, to tell you that 'it worked'. Just that." She shrugged, and went on briskly, "Something worked. She didn't say what. But I know she would have wanted to thank you for being such a good friend. She doesn't make friends easily, you know. And I'm sure she'll write soon, and by next fall everything will be back to normal. Won't that be nice?"

I slipped the necklace out of my pocket as I left, setting it carefully down next to the telephone on the hall table. Then I let myself out.

On Friday nights Mr. C always stays over and now the weather is warmer they like to sit out on the deck and cook things like shrimp and talk about taking a trip together. I'm never sure if I'm included. But of course, now that the weather is warmer. all the windows are wide open, and I can hear them better than normal.

She said:	She was a cesarean. Rory. I'm wondering if the fact she never had to fight to be born means she's more...
He said:	I don't think that causes low brain function.
She said:	She was asleep when they put her in my arms. She was born sleeping.
He said:	I think you have to face the fact it's neurological.
She said:	But what about all these vaccinations they get now, dose after dose? I've read...
He said:	Come on, now you know that's paranoid bullshit...
She said:	Is it? What if it's all my fault?
He said:	What if it's in the family? What about that autistic brother of yours? Or maybe she fell and hit her head. Who

	didn't? Maybe you should stop being so resistant and stupid…
She said:	Don't you be calling me stupid now! You don't have children. You don't know anything. This is the saddest spring I've ever lived!
He said:	Fine, well, guess what? It's no fun for me either! I'm sick and tired of talking about her and nothing but her!

He slammed back into the house, and I heard the jingle of his car keys as he picked them up. Then the cough of his car engine. Then he was gone.

His toothbrush was in the bathroom for a couple of days after that and then that was gone, too.

June 1st: What if, deep down, my mother wishes she had never had me?

CHAPTER TWENTY-THREE

I've started avoiding my mother. I'm afraid of what she's going to say. Because maybe Mr. C was on to something. Maybe I'm not "right." Like that uncle who was a baby, who died.

This morning, I went down to the basement to look for my gel pen which of course I'd lost somewhere. That's when I saw her hugging my sweatshirt as she took it out of the dryer. I couldn't find the pen.

And then after lunch when I went back into my room she was sitting on the edge of my bed. She must have just made it because it was all smooth and I'd forgotten to do it again. She was reading the journal. My journal. There isn't much in it, I know, but when I saw the look on her face my hands and feet suddenly got very cold.

"What is The Game?" she asked, closing the book gently.

I wanted to tell her. But I couldn't.

She watched me for a moment. "Maybe you'll tell me later." And she moved so I could sit on the bed with her. She pointed to the small glass jar with six sides that the honey had been in. It was on the shelf on the headboard and still had some dead flowers in it from the shrine. I thought she was going to tell me off for leaving it there, but she didn't.

"Mrs. Harvey, next door once told me that if bees are put into the bottom of a glass jar they can't get out, even if the lid is off."

"Why?"

"They don't see that it's open. Because they don't look up." She helped me lie back and get comfortable and tucked the duvet around me.

When I was little, she used to massage my stomach. Just very gently in slow circles. It was the only place I've ever really liked her touching me. She used to talk about how we were both still connected. I wished she would ask me if I wanted her to do it now, but I knew I was too old. From now on I guess I will always be too old.

"I hate everything," I said finally.

"Well, you could." She nodded. "You could do that."

"What if I hate myself, too?"

"You're changing, that's all. We've both changed. We can't go back to the way we were before."

"But I can't do anything."

"You teach me something new every day, you don't know. You are a teacher just by being here." And then she whispered, "What can I do to help? Please tell me."

I didn't answer. A tiny spider was crawling through the fine hairs on her arm. I concentrated on it and to see if I could make it turn around and head down instead of up. And it did.

She noticed it when it reached her wrist and she opened her palm to let the spider tiptoe onto it. "Now my Mum would have called that a money spider."

"Why?

"He's making my palm itch, and that means money's coming. So, I think he's telling me it'll be alright if I take a little break from work. Maybe even rent out the house and go back to Ireland for a few weeks. Maybe for the whole summer."

"Why?"

She looked pleased suddenly. "You know you just asked me "why?" for two questions in a row?"

"I did?" But my own lips were twitching because I'd asked that last one on purpose to make her smile. And she did.

She let the spider gently off onto the headboard and then rested one of her hands in the other. "Oh."

"What?"

"When I take this hand in my other one, it feels so much like my mother's hand. It feels like I'm holding it. Isn't that lovely?"

I tried it but it didn't work for me because my hands are still too small. But my skin did feel like hers.

"Can we really go?"

"Yes. Why not? We'll make friends with all of the relatives."

"Even Aunt Nuula?"

"Absolutely. Life should be like a house with all the windows brightly lit."

"What's Ireland like? Are there lots of trees?"

"Not so many trees. There are mysterious pools, though. Deep ones. There was a girl from our village went swimming in one once and we never heard from her again until she wrote from New York to ask us to send her clothes."

Since she got me to laugh, she gave me a squeeze and I noticed that her hair looked tired and tangled which it usually isn't. Or maybe I haven't noticed in a while. I hate having my hair being brushed but my mother loves it.

"If I got your brush," I managed. "I could brush your hair." That one wasn't a real question, but she smiled as if it were.

"Oh. I'd like that."

And while I went to her room to get the brush she called out, "And you have some cousins there, about your age, but I think you may be a lot more mature than they are."

My mother says a lot of things. Sometimes she talks too much, but I loved it when she said that.

It's getting sunny now and sometimes the sun hurts my eyes. My mother says it's not very sunny in Ireland, but that people are made of quite bright colors so you don't notice. I used to think my mother was made of stronger colors than me, but yesterday when I was crying, and there were still tears on my lashes, I looked through them and I could see tiny rainbows - so I think there must be real, bright colors in me somewhere.

June 3rd: I have to tell the bees I'm leaving. And I have to tell them about the jar – that the lid is open, and all they have to do is look up.

About the Author

Christine Foster's award-winning plays have been produced in the US, Canada, Mexico, Australia, New Zealand, UK, Europe and Asia. She has written dozens of TV scripts for the Canadian Broadcasting Corp., History Channel and the Family Channel. As well, she has had many pieces appear in newspapers and esteemed periodicals.

Christine is the mother of a neurodivergent adult daughter from whom she has learned more than she can say. *The Lemon Golf Diary* is her first novel.

For more info: christinefoster.ca

Printed in Dunstable, United Kingdom